REDMOND O'HANLON'S
Into the Heart of Borneo

"Simultaneously terrifying and hilarious."   —*Vogue*

"Among all the hilarity and laughs there's enough substance to make for an uncommon travel book."   —*Booklist*

"*Into the Heart of Borneo* is a serious account of O'Hanlon and Fenton's 1983 journey...but it is also, as its mock-heroic title suggests, a lively account of two overgrown boys on a B-movie adventure....The jungle is ...extraordinarily beautiful as well as funny....*Into the Heart of Borneo* is a delightful book."   —*New York*

"Mr. O'Hanlon vividly describes the astonishing birds that flutter through the trees and the equally colorful and sadly frail humans."   —*Wall Street Journal*

"The real stars of this Monty Python-esque road show are the Iban guides who think these guys are too old and fat to be believed, but shepherd them with sweet attention."   —*Vogue*

"O'Hanlon can write with great delicacy. For all his whimsy, he shows remarkable awareness of the feelings of their Iban companions and of the tribesmen they meet along the way."   —*Los Angeles Times*

"O'Hanlon is a very literate writer. He is also very funny....Wry wit and style seldom grace travel stories. But they do in this work, which is, in essence, an artfully linked collection of often hilarious road adventures. ...Oh, what a lovely treat!"   —*San Diego Union*

By the same author
JOSEPH CONRAD AND CHARLES DARWIN

IN TROUBLE AGAIN

NO MERCY

VINTAGE DEPARTURES

REDMOND O'HANLON

INTO THE HEART OF BORNEO

VINTAGE BOOKS

A DIVISION OF RANDOM HOUSE, NEW YORK

Library of Congress Cataloging-in-Publication Data

O'Hanlon, Redmond, 1947–
Into the heart of Borneo.

(Vintage departures)
Bibliography: p.
Includes index.
1. Borneo—Description and travel.
2. O'Hanlon, Redmond, 1947– —Journeys—Borneo.
3. Fenton, James, 1949– —Journeys—Borneo.
I. Title.
[DS646.3.O44   1987]   915.98'30438   87-40084
ISBN 0-394-75540-5 (pbk.)

A portion of this work was originally published in *Granta*, London.

To my wife, Belinda

The author wishes to thank 22 SAS;
Eric Jacobs and the *Sunday Times*;
Bill Buford and *Granta*; Galen Strawson;
Ernst Mayr; Max Peterson; Linda Hopkins;
and Fuji Cameras (UK) Ltd.

INTO THE HEART OF BORNEO

INTO
THE
HEART
OF
BORNEO

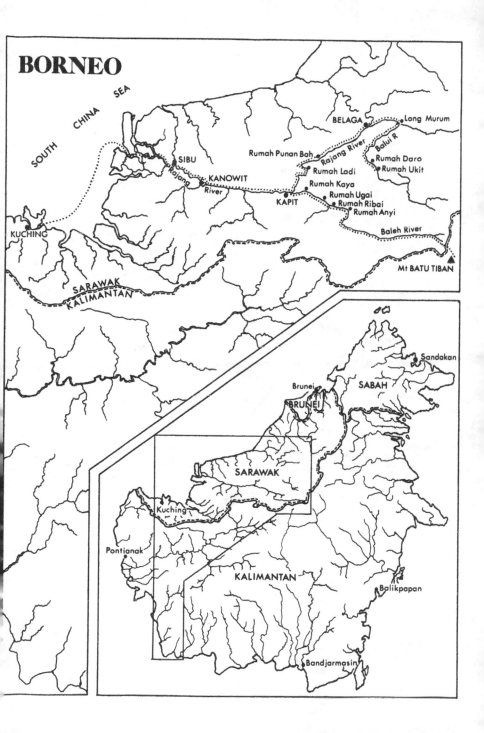

· ONE ·

The situation in Sarawak as seen by Haddon in 1888 is still much the same today. He found a series of racial strata moving downwards in society and backwards in time as he moved inwards on the island.

C. D. Darlington, *The Evolution of Man and Society*, 1969

As a former academic and a natural history book reviewer I was astonished to discover, on being threatened with a two-month exile to the primary jungles of Borneo, just how fast a man can read.

Powerful as your scholarly instincts may be, there is no matching the strength of that irrational desire to find a means of keeping your head upon your shoulders; of retaining your frontal appendage in its accustomed place; of barring 1,700 different species of parasitic worm from your bloodstream and Wagler's pit viper from just about anywhere; of removing small, black, wild-boar ticks from your crutch with minimum discomfort (you do it with Sellotape); of declining to wear a globulating necklace of leeches all day long; of sidestepping amoebic and bacillary dysentery, yellow and blackwater and dengue fevers, malaria, cholera, typhoid, rabies, hepatitis, tuberculosis and the crocodile (thumbs in its eyes, if you have time, they say).

A rubber suit, with a pair of steel waders, seemed the obvious answer. But then the temperature runs to 95 °F in the shade, and the humidity is 98 per cent. Hose and McDougall's great two-volume masterpiece *The Pagan Tribes of Borneo* (1912), Alfred Russel Wallace's *The Malay Archipelago: the Land of the Orang-Utan and the Bird of Paradise* (2 vols, 1869; a book even richer than its title indicates), Odoardo Beccari's *Wanderings in the Great Forests of Borneo* (1904), Hose's *The Field-book of a Jungle-Wallah* (1929) and Robert Shelford's *A Naturalist in Borneo* (1916) offered no immediate solution. And then meek, dead, outwardly unimpressive, be-suited and bowler-hatted Uncle Eggy came to my rescue.

Reading Tom Harrisson's memoirs of the war against the Japanese in Borneo, *World Within* (1959), I came across the following passage. Harrisson, sent out of his own unit on a secret mission, faces his selector:

> In the relics of a Northumberland Avenue hotel, I was inter-viewed by Colonel Egerton-Mott . . . Mott offered me Borneo . . . adding that I was about the last of their hopes. They had already (he said) asked everyone with any conceivable knowledge of the country, including my colleagues of the 1932 Oxford expedition. When I practically leapt at the offer, he shed his cavalry veneer of calm for a second in pleased evident relief. For, in a tiny way, the British services at that moment badly needed to find a few men to go back into Borneo and try to save some of the face, chin-up, lost to the Japanese.
>
> For the next few weeks my lately softening feet hardly felt ground. Special Operations Executive, "SOE", the British centre of cloak-and-dagger, was a most efficient organisation, in a different class from the ordinary army or civilian services. Parachuting, coding, disguise, hiding, searching, tailing, burglaring, stealing trains, blowing up railway bridges, sham-ming deafness, passing on syphilis, resisting pain, firing from the hip, forgery and the interruption of mail, were some things one could learn in intense concentration. None of them would be of much use in the east. But the acquisition of so much criminal and lethal knowledge gave a kick of self-confidence.

So now, at last, I knew how my mild-mannered uncle had really spent his time, the nature of that "something in the City" and those "interests in the East" of which my aunt would speak with such disdain. Armed with my newly-revealed ancestor, I decided to seek help from the intellectual descendants of the Special Operations Executive.

The training area of 22 SAS near Hereford is the best place on earth from which to begin a journey upriver into the heart of the jungle. The nearest I had ever come to a tropical rain-forest, after all, was in the Bodleian Library, via the pages of the great nineteenth-century traveller-naturalists, Humboldt, Darwin, Wallace, Bates, Thomas Belt—and, in practice, a childhood spent rabbiting in the Wiltshire woods. My companion James Fenton, however, whose idea the venture was, enigmatic, balding, an ex-correspondent of the war in Vietnam and Cambodia, a jungle in himself, was a wise old man in these matters.

Still, as the gates swung open from a remote control point in the guardroom and our camouflaged Land Rover climbed the small track across the fields, even James was unnerved by the view. Booby-trapped lorries and burnt-out vehicles littered the landscape; displaced lines of turf disclosed wires running in all directions; from Neolithic-seeming earthworks, there came the muffled hammering of silenced small-arms fire; impossibly burly hippies in Levi jeans and trendy sweaters piled out of a truck like fragments of a hand-grenade and disappeared into the grass; mock-up streets and shuttered embassies went past, and then, as we drove round a fold in the hill, an airliner appeared, sitting neatly in a field of wheat.

"What's that?" said James.

Malcolm and Eddy forebore to reply.

We drew up by a fearsome assault course (the parallel bars you are supposed to scramble over with enthusiasm reared into the sky like a dockside crane) and made our way into the local SAS jungle. Apart from the high wire perimeter fence, the frequency with which Land Rovers drove past, the number of helicopters overhead and the speed with which persons unknown were discharging revolvers from a place whose exact position it was impossible to ascertain, it might have been a wood in England.

"What a pity," said Malcolm, "that you can't come to Brunei with us for a week. We could really sort you out and set you up over there."

"What a pity," I agreed, moistening with sweat at the very thought.

"Some people just can't hack the jungle at all," said Eddy.

"Now," said Malcolm, taking a small green package out of the newly-designed Bergen back-pack, "it's all very simple. You find two trees eight feet apart where there's no evidence of any silt on the ground—the rivers can rise eighteen feet overnight and you don't want to drown in a wet dream, do you? Check the tree trunks for termites. Termites mean dead branches and dead branches, sooner or later, mean dead men. We lost a lot of men like that, in storms at night. Tie these cords round the trees, put these metal stiffeners across each end like this, and there's your hammock. If the CT [Communist Terrorists] are very good, they can pick you up by the cord marks on the bark, so brush them down in the morning. Now—here's your mossie net and you just tie it over your hammock and peg it out by these strings to the surrounding bushes until it forms a good tight box like that—and you really want to watch it, because malaria pills only give you 30 per cent protection. Here's your top cover—take some tape in case it tears round those eye-holes; mine always did after two or three months—and that's it; there's your genuine basha."

A long green tube had materialised above the brambles in front of us, seemingly in a minute or two.

"Stop around three or four in the afternoon," said Malcolm, "give yourself plenty of time. Light one of these blocks that makes no smoke and boil up a cup of tea. And just sit by your tree until dark if the enemy are about. Now—who's going to test it?"

I looked hard at James.

James looked hard at a bush.

The hammock was about five feet off the ground. So this was it, the first piece of action, day one . . . Darwin, I remembered, had had excruciating problems trying to get into his hammock, but I just could not quite recall how he had solved them. I took in a great deal of air, which is how the grouper fish breaks surface, and got airborne backwards. Nets, ropes, parachute cords, canvas sheets and metal stiffener rods strung me up from throat to ankles.

"It's a good job the trees are young and fit, anyway," said Eddy, "or you'd have brought the whole lot down on us."

Back at the quartermaster's stores we signed for our new kit. One Silvo and one prismatic compass (black and heavy as a little bomb in its canvas belt-case); two parangs—thick knives eighteen inches long which had chopped and slashed their way through the Indonesian confrontation from 1962 to 1966; torches; belts; pouches; powders; insect repellents; parachute cord; water bottles; water purifying tablets; stoves; fuel blocks; mess-tins; the complete basha equipment and rations enough (Menu C) for three patrols moving in groups of four for three weeks.

It was Test Week at Hereford—the final week of the selection course during which the SAS take their pick of the eager volunteers from other regiments, and as we piled up our booty a young man with glazed eyes walked silently in, deposited his compass on the counter, and left.

"He's done well," said Malcolm. "No messing there. He's the first back today. Forty-five miles over the Beacons. Fifty-pound Bergen. Twelve-pound belt kit. Eighteen-pound rifle. If you add in the hills it works out at three marathons on the trot, so they say." I was glad we were merely going to the jungle.

"Good luck lads," said Malcolm, sending us off to see the Major in charge of the Training Wing. "We've left a lot of men in Borneo— know what I mean?"

The soft-spoken Major, veteran of Special Forces campaigns in occupied Europe in the Second World War, of the war in Malaya, of Jebel Akhdar, Aden, Borneo and Dhofar, was huge. It was vastly reassuring to think that so much muscle could actually squeeze itself into a jungle and come out again undiminished. And his office, hung with battle honours, Special Air Service shields emblazoned with the Regiment's motto, *Qui ose gagne*; with a mass of wall charts documenting the progress of his latest candidates; with cartoons of all the wrong ways to resist interrogation; and libraried with strictly practical works in natural history—on edible fungi, on traps and tracking and poaching, on different recipes for the cooking of rats and instructions on the peeling of cockroaches—was an impressive place. Determined young men stared down on us from the line of group photographs of each year's successful applicants. Several of them, I noticed, had two diagonal lines drawn across their bodies with a felt-tip pen. In just one helicopter crash in the Falklands eighteen men had been drowned: the regiment's largest single loss since 1945.

"You'll find the high spot of your day," said the Major, "is cleaning your teeth. The only bit of you you can keep clean. Don't shave in the jungle, because the slightest nick turns septic at once. And don't take more than one change of clothes, because you must keep your Bergen weight well down below sixty pounds. And don't expect your Iban trackers to carry it for you, either, because they have enough to do transporting their own food. So keep one set of dry kit in a sealed bag in your pack. Get into that each night after you've eaten. Powder yourself all over, too, with zinc talc—don't feel sissy about it—you'll halve the rashes and the rot and the skin fungus. Then sleep. Then get up at five thirty and into your wet kit. It's uncomfortable at first, but don't weaken—ever; if you do, there'll be two sets of wet kit in no time, you'll lose sleep and lose strength and then there'll be a disaster. But take as many dry socks as you can. Stuff them into all the crannies in your pack. And, in the morning, soak the pairs you are going to wear in Autan insect repellent, to keep the leeches out of your boots. Stick it on your arms and round your waist and neck and in your hair, too, while you're about it, but not on your forehead because the sweat carries it into your eyes and it stings. Cover yourself at night, too, against the mosquitoes. Take them seriously, because malaria is a terrible thing and it's easy to get, pills or no.

"Get some jungle boots, good thick trousers and strong shirts. You won't want to nancy about in shorts once the first leech has had a go at you, believe me. Acclimatise slowly. The tropics takes people in different ways. Fit young men may pass out top here and then just collapse in Brunei. You'll think it's the end of the world. You can't breathe. You can't move. And then after two weeks you'll be used to it. And once in the jungle proper you'll never want to come out.

"It's a beautiful country and the Iban are a fine people. I was on the Bavam myself, but to go up the Rajang and the Baleh will be better for your purposes. That's a good plan. The Baleh is very seldom visited, if at all, upriver, and the Tiban mountains should be very wild indeed. They look small on a map, those mountains, but they're tough going. One steep hill after another. And you have to be good with a compass. Any questions? No. Good. Well done, lads, Goodbye and good luck."

James and I drove out past the guardroom and the police post in a stunned silence, the back of the car bristling with serious, dark-green and camouflage-brown equipment; and we fell into the King's Arms. Some hours later we found ourselves in the cathedral, mutely surveying the Mappa Mundi, drawn on vellum by Richard of Haldingham c 1300. Jerusalem was there all right, plum in the centre; Borneo was nowhere to be seen; but its inhabitants, for all we and Richard of Haldingham knew, had strayed across his big brown chart of the earth; there they were: the *Philli* ("test the chastity of their wives by exposing their new-born children to serpents"), the *Phanesii* ("are covered with the skin of their ears. A bat-like people with enormous drooping ears") and the *Essendones* ("it is their custom to carry out the funeral of their parents with singing and collecting a company of friends to devour the actual corpses with their teeth"). Was it time to stay at home?

• TWO •

There remained but one obvious authority to consult, John Hatt, author of *The Tropical Traveller* (1982), the modern equivalent of Francis Galton's *The Art of Travel; or, Shifts and Contrivances Available in Wild Countries* (1855).

For a man who had been everywhere Hatt seemed far too young, until I realised, with some misgivings on our own account, that the speed and force with which he both talked and Dunlop-green-flashed about the room in his gym shoes was a genuine expression of his genetic make-up; and that a circumnavigation of the globe once a week at the double would probably pose him no particular problem.

"Let me see," said Hatt, skydiving towards his sofa and collecting a notebook from a table in mid-flight. "Oh yes—take *lots* of postcards of the Queen, preferably on horseback, and showing all four legs, because they think she's all of a piece. And for the Headmen, packets of salt and aginomoto, sarongs, waterproof digital watches. For yourselves—Hatt's tips for travellers—those sealable transparent document bags, Tubigrip bandage for every part of your anatomy and, as well as your jungle boots, gym shoes. Because in the long-houses you will have to dance every night. It's simply impossible to refuse. Three or four girls will come and pull you up and then you have to do your thing in front of the assembled tribe—just twenty minutes or so. No problem really. And then you must sing, of course. Why not learn a duet? A duet would be splendid, absolutely splendid. The lives of the primitive farmers are pretty monotonous, after all, and isolated and lonely when they are staying out in their huts on the hill-padi fields, so when they are in the longhouse together they snatch any chance to have a party, and you'll provide a good excuse. You're expected to entertain them in any way you can; and you're also expected to get very drunk indeed. Rice-wine, tuak, is deceptively mild, and rice-brandy, arak, is every bit as lethal as it tastes. There's really no escape. Even where you're flat out on the floor, when the bundles of heads in their rattan nets start to jiggle about and wink at you, you're not off the hook. The girls hold your nose; and when you open your mouth to breathe they tip in another glass or two. Then you'll discover just how arak can supercharge an ordinary nightmare. I used to dream that I'd wake up with a palang."

"A palang?" we asked, uneasily.

"Oh, it's quite a simple little operation, really," said Hatt, "although sepsis is always a problem. They clamp the penis in an instrument that looks like a small bow; and then drive a six-inch nail through it, just beneath the glans."

"Hang on," said Fenton.

"No—it's perfectly true," said Hatt, darting at his bookshelves like a kingfisher into the water. "I can even give you a reference. Here we are. How's that? The *Sarawak Museum Journal* volume VII, December 1956. It's a by-the-way in an article by Tom Harrisson on the Borneo rhinoceros:

"One of the exhibits that excites the most interest in our museum is that of the *palang*. This is the tube or rod of bamboo, bone, hardwood, etc. with which the end of the penis is pierced among many inland people, principally the Indonesian Kenyahs, but also many others—and lately even spreading to the Kelabits in the uplands. In each end of this centre-piece may be attached knobs, points or even blades of suitable material. Some men have two *palang*, at right angles through the penis tip.

"The function of this device is, superficially, to add to the sexual pleasure of the women by stimulating and extending the inner walls of the vagina. It is, in this, in my experience decidedly successful.

"We also have a 'natural' *palang*, exhibited alongside. This is the penis of a Borneo rhinoceros. In the natural state this powerful piece of the anatomy has, about four inches behind the tip, a similar sort of cross-bar, projecting nearly two inches out on each side. When tense, this becomes a fairly rigid bar, much like the human *palang* in general implication. The one we have on show in the Museum has had a hardwood rod fixed in it (to keep it rigid). As such, these things were included among the *esoterica* of inland longhouses, along with sacred stones, beads, strange teeth and other charms used mainly in connection with human head and fertility ceremonies.

"Many who have handled this pachyderm device have been unable to credit that it is 'genuine'. However, in the untouched state it can be even more impressive. The penis of another male (with not full-size horn) in our possession measures over a foot and a half (relaxed), has a longer tip and cross-piece than the Museum's displayed one . . .

"Well," said Hatt, helpfully, "if Harrisson can have it done, I don't see why you shouldn't. And I'd be grateful if you could test two other little ideas of mine: could one of you take massive doses of vitamin B1 (thiamine) at about three o'clock every afternoon? And then let me know if it keeps off the mosquitoes?"

"Do we make a comparative count of bites? Or will the first to get malaria decide the issue?"

"Yes, yes—either will do. And could you get your chemist to make this up? It's a possible new repellent."

Hatt handed Fenton a page of notebook on which was inscribed:

2—EPHYL—1—3—HEXANDIOL 846. gr/1
and N,N—DIETHYL—M—TOLUMIDE 95/gr/1

"But Hatt," said Fenton, "how do we know that this isn't dynamite?"

THREE

At Singapore airport, carrying my Smith and Wesson, well wrapped in its cardboard box, a Malay policeman escorted me through the luxurious corridors of the new building towards the Customs Strong-room.

"Why you travel with a gun?"

"Well," I said, "we're going to try and reach the Tiban mountains in the very centre of Borneo. Up the Rajang river. Up the Baleh to its source; and then we'll march through the primary jungle. No one's been since Mjoberg in 1926—and he went in from the other side. Besides, there just might be a Borneo rhinoceros or two still about on the higher slopes. Who knows?"

"You go just to see rhinoceros?" the policeman said, appalled. "But they eat people in there! They're cannibals! Blowpipes! Phut. Phut. You die. No noise. Very better than a gun."

I must not, I thought, tell James, who, as a hard-working man, was in any case all for a little holiday snorkelling over the northern coral reefs, a stroll up the pretty Mount Kinabalu in Sabah and a visit to the eastern island of Bum-Bum-Tutu. Surrounded by sympathetic officials, I deposited the Smith and Wesson for the night.

When I returned, James was talking to the official in charge of airport security.

"Hey, Redmond, my friend here says that in the middle of Borneo they're all cannibals still. We are going to be eaten."

"Oh, nonsense," I said, "but let's have a few more drinks, just in case."

In Raffles that night I cheered myself up with a secret re-read of the introduction of Smythies's great classic *The Birds of Borneo*, in which he remarks that "Borneo is the third largest island in the world, after

Greenland and New Guinea, and five times the area of England and Wales. It is one enormous forest. Estimates prepared by the Forest Departments from aerial photographs show that 75 per cent of the island is under primary forest, and a further 10 to 15 per cent under secondary forest." The "general picture . . . is of a central mountain chain, or spinal range, running down the middle of the island (axis NE–SW), and throwing off several long spurs like the arms of a starfish. Towards the coast there are often extensive lowlands, and also flat swampy areas associated with the estuaries of the larger rivers . . . From Mt Murud to Mt Batu-Tibang the spinal chain is inaccessible and little known, and has been reached or crossed by Europeans at a limited number of points only; its exact position on the map is not known to within 20 miles, no points on it having been fixed by triangulation or star observations."

We came into the little airport at Kuching over the slack muddy windings of the Sarawak river, the mangrove swamps, the stretch of forest broken only by outcrops of ochre rock. On the tarmac, crossing to the airport sheds, the heat of the equator hit me for the first time. It squeezed round you like the rank coils of an unseen snake, pressing the good air out of your lungs, covering you in a slimy sweat. Fifteen yards of this was enough; a mile would be impossible; five hundred miles an absurdity.

"How do you like it?" said James.

"Wonderful," I replied, smiling through the coils, trying to breathe.

Between the drops of sweat that ran off my forehead and over my glasses I could just make out an enormous notice on the wall of the customs shack. "10,000 YEARS" (or thereabouts) it proclaimed. "FOR THOSE CARRYING SMITH AND WESSONS."

"Why you bring gun?" asked the Malay officer, with a weary grin.

"It's—er—for shooting wild pig."

"No, no. It's because you think we all just down from the trees here. You think only England civilised country."

"Er—not at all—this is a wonderful country."

"Very true, my friend. So you not need gun. I take it for store. You make British Council write for you. We let you take it away—when you go away."

Much ashamed, I watched the departure of my oily, shiny, black companion.

"Don't fret," said James, thoroughly relieved, but in the tone of voice he might adopt to comfort a toddler whose lollipop had just been nicked, "we'll find you something equally nasty. A really big bow and arrow—something like that."

"But don't you understand? This means we'll have to go in with just our dicks in our hands!"

"And a good thing too. You'll be altogether calmer with your dick in your hand."

A Malay taxi driver agreed to take us into Kuching, to a cheap lodging house. Even suburban nature seemed aggressively lush, rampant with excessively large palms; with trees covered with ferns, ferns like fans, ferns sprouting like bullrushes in every fork of every tree. The roadside undergrowth was neck high. Some of the outlying Malay houses were built on stilts, the odd monkey swinging idly beneath the bases of the houses.

It was Chinese New Year, and all the shops in the little streets were shuttered and locked. Mangy dogs, a little like African wild dogs, but with droopy ears, lay in the shade of the alleyways. And there were tiny cats, too, each one seemingly docked at the tail. Robert Shelford, Curator of Rajah Brooke's Sarawak Museum from 1897 to 1904 and a world authority on *Blattidae*, the cockroaches, was obviously a man to trust in small matters. The Borneo cat, he writes, is possessed of "large ears and a body so short and hindlegs so long that it altogether lacks the sinuous grace which even the most mongrel English Grimalkin exhibits. The tail is either an absurd twisted knot or else very short and terminating in a knob; this knotting of the tail is caused by a natural dislocation of the vertebrae so that they join on to each other at all sorts of angles."

We took two rooms in the lodging house which, in the absence of its Chinese owners, was staffed by very young, very sleepy, very friendly Land Dyaks. It was easy to see why the Rajahs Brooke considered them to be the least enterprising, the least troublesome of all the peoples in the territory. Our four attendants lay peacefully around the tiny reception desk, one on the floor, one on a sofa, and two in chairs. It made one yawn just to look at them. In fact everything seemed calm and easeful, and as it should be. Shutting my door, I was undisturbed by a cockroach, as big as a mouse and markedly faster on its feet, which shot out from under the bed, brown-blurred its way across the linoleum and swung a right through the door of the bathroom partition. Following along behind, I was not disgusted by the stray faeces which lay on the tiles and which had obviously escaped from the combined shower and lavatory exit hole in the corner. The cockroach must have gone that way, so presumably all could still be partially lost through the remaining passage. A gecko was enjoying itself, amplifying its chirps from a singing post somewhere in an overflow pipe. Bored mosquitoes drifted in and out of the broken window. Palm trees grew opposite, and someone had built a hut with a corrugated iron roof in the grounds of a large, ruined, English-colonial house. The squatter was growing maize where, presumably, a lawn had once stretched down to the road. Lush, tangled scrub grew round the edges of his little plantation. As I watched, a bird that looked like a magpie flew like a thrush, perched in a tree to my right, and began to sing, like a robin. The sweat trickled down my back. I decided to take a siesta.

I took the third edition of Bertram E. Smythies's *The Birds of Borneo* out of my Bergen. I found the black, white and blue bird on plate XXXI. It was a Magpie-robin: my first positive identification of a Borneo bird. Turn to page 300, said the key, for its description. It so happens, as I know now, that a printer's error has eliminated all trace of the full-page discussion of the Magpie-robin from the third edition of Smythies, by entering a double heading for the Rufous-tailed shama, *Copsychus pyrropyga* (Lesson) 1839. I decided that this tiny, sinister mystery did not worry me, either.

I put Smythies aside and lay back on the bed. A fusillade of Chinese fire-crackers went off in the street on the other side of the lodging house, followed by sharp single reports, like snipers' shots. I shut my eyes, and then opened them again. I was startled to see my tutor from undergraduate days at Oxford, fifteen years before, the kindly John Jones, standing at the end of the bed. His large head was unaccountably swollen to the size of a hundredweight sack; his eyes bulged like light bulbs. He put his knuckles on the mattress and leaned forward. "Yes, Redmond," he said, in his intense way, giving each word its full share of time in his mouth, "but what have you ever *done* in life?"

I sat up, sharply; and my tutor disappeared. I decided that I was very worried indeed. I went to the Bergen and, trembling slightly, drew out the whisky bottle.

That evening, we walked the temporarily half-deserted streets of Kuching. At the upper windows of the houses we could see Chinese families, the generations gathered, the lanterns lit, celebrating the beginning of the Year of the Pig. The occasional very old man, invariably with his very young grandson beside him, loitering in a downstairs doorway, impassively admiring the opposite rooftops, taking the evening air, would flick a fire-cracker under our feet as we passed.

On the larger buildings, above the neon signs and fairy-lights, roosting White-bellied swiftlets chattered to each other from every ledge. We wandered down to the waterfront where small cargo ships were moored, near the quay where James Brooke first landed.

An ex-officer in the Indian Army, an English gentleman-adventurer with a private income and a private yacht, Brooke, inspired by the career of Sir Stamford Raffles, the founder of Singapore, arrived in Sarawak in 1839. The local ruler, Pengiran Muda Hasim, a prince of the Sultanate of Brunei which held nominal sovereign power over northern Borneo (the Dutch governed the south and south-east of the island from a rich base in Java) was hopelessly entangled in civil war against a coalition of local tribes: Brooke, with great courage and panache, led Hasim's men against the rebels, won the war, and demanded and received the province of "Sarawak Proper" (roughly the area included in the modern state's First Division) as his reward. He then, with initial British naval support, cleared his coasts of Malay-led Sea Dyak pirates (the Malays traditionally kept the goods, and the Sea Dyaks the heads, of their victims) and extended his influence up the major rivers. Thereafter, the Foreign Office refused to be interested in Brooke's impoverished kingdom and in 1868 the embittered old man bequeathed his private country to his nephew and successor, Charles Brooke. Charles, tough, austere, his idea of his role as Rajah formed partly by an arduous early career in hazardous outstations in his uncle's service, partly by his assumption of the social attitudes of the Victorian squirearchy, governed Sarawak for fifty years like a country gentleman managing his estates. Charles died in 1917 and was succeeded by his son, Vyner Brooke, a man who liked his rank but disliked the administrative duties that went with it. After Pearl Harbor the Japanese relieved him of both; and, when the war was over, feeling unequal to the burden of re-building, Vyner Brooke ceded his state to the British Crown. In 1963 Sarawak joined Malaya, Singapore and Sabah (British North Borneo) to form the Federation of Malaysia (from which Singapore was expelled in 1965).

In general, the history of Brooke rule in Sarawak is one of paternalistic benevolence, of a protective legislation marred only by the frequent use of Sea Dyak levies on punitive expeditions which were intended to keep the peace, but which also licensed head-hunting and founded enduring dynasties of blood feuds. But then there was no alternative, no money to pay for a regular, disciplined army (the Sarawak Rangers were a tiny force). No one could accuse the White Rajahs of exploiting the peoples in their kingdom (there was not much to exploit).

Which is probably why, in the long view, a deaf-mute Malay suddenly felt impelled to sidle out of the shadow of a warehouse wall and shake us both by the hand. He made curious grunting noises, as if attempting to clear his throat of phlegm without result. We set off up the waterfront road towards the Chinese temple on a hillock at its head. The deaf-mute padded along behind us. In the almost empty street a flashing sign drew us towards its housefront: "SNACK BAR SNACK BAR SNACK BAR" it said. James mounted the stairs, I followed, and our companion waited in the street.

"Good evening," I heard James say, as he reached the top, and then "Oh I see, so you're a brothel."

We fled down the stairs. The deaf-mute, much excited, was jumping up and down, pointing at his penis.

"Yes, spot on," said James, pointing at his mouth, "but we're hungry." We all three opened our mouths, like birds in a nest.

The deaf-mute led us up the street, past the Chinese temple, along a broad road that followed the bend of the Sarawak river to a new cluster of Singapore-style modern concrete buildings. And there, to our traveller's disgust, to our actual delight in the presence of all the nastiness we were supposed to have left behind, stood the Holiday Inn, Kuching. Our guide waved goodbye and walked back towards the town.

"James," I said warily, over the cognac, "how's your dream-life been? Did you have a siesta? Did you sleep this afternoon? Did you?"

"Just a bit," said James, "yes. I had a zizz. I read a little. I made some lists—we must remember to take cigarette lighters. And at least five cartons of ciggies."

"But did you dream?"

"I had a dream or two. The odd dreamette. Why? What's the matter with you?"

"Well—my old tutor called to see me. I sat up and he disappeared."

"Oh, that's simple," said James, grinning. "You wish to kill your father."

"Don't be silly. Didn't you have a nightmare, too? What did you dream about?"

"As it happens," said James, "I am much troubled by a leering Chinaman. But it's nothing to worry about. It's a common occurrence when you first come to the equator. The brain just cannot believe its own dials. It sits there and looks at its instrument panel and it says to itself 'Hang on. We couldn't possibly have lost all that sweat from the tanks. And the temperature gauge has bust a thermometer. I don't believe it'; and so the brain crash-lands itself, and then your old tutor pays a call. He's got a name, your old tutor. He's called a hypnagogic vision. But you soon recover."

In bed that night, to outwit the hypnagogic visions, I covered myself in SAS insect repellent and read one of the notebooks I had compiled in Oxford. Under Kuching, in one section, I had extracted the following information from C.P. Law's paper "Chinese Temples in Kuching—II", in the Sarawak Museum Journal, vol IX, July-December 1959: the temple we had passed belonged to

Sea San Ten . . . or Tua Pek Kong Keng . . . of the Chou Dynasty. He is, in effect, the "Mayor" of Kuching in the Chinese spiritual sense, just as each city has its mayor of this sort. Whenever anyone dies, the relatives come here to report the death. And by each grave in the cemetery there is a miniature grave to the god, at which offering is first made before worshipping the ancestor. This god was born on the second day of the second moon and died on the fifteenth day of the eighth moon. The temple was erected here 83 years ago, at first an atap shed, now a carved and ornamented small building . . . The second oldest Kuching Temple is that in Carpenter Street, sponsored by the Teochew community. It was built 62 years ago in honour of Hian Tien Shian Tee . . . "God of Heaven", who was born on the third day of the third moon, and died on the ninth day of the ninth moon. On earth he was low ranking in saintliness. He was forbidden to eat meat, but did so. When the Buddha accused him, he denied the charge. The Buddha struck him upon the back, and from his mouth emerged a turtle and a snake. At this, in shame, he cut open his stomach with a knife, and died. Partly in commemoration of this, turtles are kept in a concrete tank in the temple, some of them for many decades.

After two days of enforced rest, reading, sleeping, walking the streets, the Chinese holiday ended. The town burst into life; the shutters were rolled up; stalls were set out everywhere; personal walking-width on the pavements was reduced to two-foot-six and the 98 per cent moisture in the air was displaced by a 98 per cent saturation in droplets of cooking fat from the row of cafés in the market. Upcountry Land Dyaks spread cloths on the ground by the market square and offered bundles of unrecognisable fruit for sale. We walked in the park and admired the Tailor birds, the Pied trillers and a Common kingfisher flying across the ornamental lake. We retreated to the shade and the ordered quiet of the Kuching Museum and stared, with unspoken alarm, at stuffed specimens of the Mangrove cat snake; the Mock viper; the Grass green whip snake; the Common Malayan racer; the Cobra; the Hamadryad; the Banded krait; the Banded coral snake (long and thin as a loop of intestine) and three equally unprepossessing varieties of Wagler's pit viper. We inspected the natural palang of the Borneo rhinoceros and the unnatural palang of *Homo sapiens*: in fact a "triangular wedge of chalk-like calcine embedding in it a palang of warped iron: 21 mm in length, just over 1 mm in diameter at exposed end. Weight 26 gms." That growing wedge of chalk-like calcine deposited on the palang by the flow of urine, and itself embedded in the tissues of the penis must, we decided, have been uncomfortable. On the way out we paused to look at a hairball taken from the stomach of a crocodile, Sarawak river. It was a round mass of fibres, the size of a soccer ball, and in a small depression on its top left quadrant a handwritten note proclaimed: "Dental plate found here." We went for a gentle stroll in the gardens, to recover.

FOUR

The next morning, just before dawn, we took a taxi to the Sibu Wharf and boarded a Chinese launch full of Malay soldiers returning to their regiment. The crew cast off, the engines puttered us slowly down the Sarawak river through the rising mist, opened up with surprising power and eardrum-cracking noise across a small piece of the South China Sea and, by midday, were thrusting us into the mouth of the great Rajang. Several ocean-going timber ships passed us bound, probably, for Japan. The low, monotonous, distant banks of mangrove swamp seemed to stand still, hour after hour.

Sometime in the late afternoon I awoke, slumped in my seat, to find that we had reached Sibu. The now-wooded banks had edged to within a mile of each other; a huge sprawl of concrete buildings stretched back into the hinterland on our left; tugs backed and filled in the river, pushing and pulling log-laden barges up to the bank, and Chinese river launches clustered at the jetties. That evening, from our rooms in a Chinese hotel, we watched as, high up, black silhouettes beneath the clouds, some two hundred Brahminy kites drifted over us, flying and gliding leisurely south across the river from their feeding grounds around the rubbish tips on the outskirts of the town towards their roosts in the jungle on the opposite bank.

At five in the morning we took the last two places on the roof of a small Chinese passenger boat, squatting among the lashed empty baskets of Ibans returning to their longhouses from Sibu market, and, by mid-afternoon, having stopped at almost every settlement along the way, we arrived in Kapit, the real starting-point for our journey proper.

With our Bergens and kit-bags we toiled up the concrete steps of the upriver pier to the high bank on which Kapit stands. To our left was the small fort, its walls pierced with a single row of rifle ports, its grounds formerly displaying a few cannon. One of a number of such forts, which were an important part of the Brookes' strategy for controlling their outlying districts, Kapit is unusual in one respect: most of the other defences (apart from providing protection to a local administrative officer, a Resident) were built to stop fleets of Iban war-canoes from descending their home rivers for coastal raids. Kapit was built to prevent the Ibans from paddling *up* the Rajang and its tributary, the Baleh, either to settle beyond the reach of the government; or to go hunting for the heads of the less aggressive hill-rice farmers of the interior, the Melanau, the Kayan or the Kenyah; or to catch and decapitate the gentle hunter-gathering semi-nomads who live in the primary jungles far inland at the head of the rivers.

That was the theory, anyhow. In practice the Resident in charge of the upper Rajang station, F.D. "Minggo" de Rozario, whose father had been James Brooke's Portuguese chef in the Astana at Kuching, seemed more or less helpless, at least in the early days, to stop Iban war parties from moving in either direction. But then Rozario was himself an exception amongst Charles Brooke's senior officers. In general, to be selected for a post in the Rajah's service, you had to be an English gentleman (or thereabouts); single (no marriage permitted for at least ten years); and young (under twenty-five). Thereafter, your inner resources were expected to be extensive enough to enable you to live for years without need of European friends, your intellect good enough to allow you to master the local language and the local law, and your natural instincts vigorous enough to compel you to take a native mistress (but not to take her with you on government steamers).

Charles Brooke socially manipulated far more than the lives of his immediate juniors; he permanently rearranged the interrelations of his subject peoples according to his own odd convictions. The evidence was all around us as we walked in a downstream direction from Kapit fort towards the Rajang Hotel. Clustered nearest the fort was the Chinese bazaar, once a simple row of shops, now three sides of a square and several streets as well. Brooke encouraged the Chinese to trade: that was their role; he helped them set up shop (but no Chinaman was allowed to trade directly in a longhouse, where his measures could not be checked and the Iban might be cheated); he let them dominate the river traffic; he even blessed Foochow Christian immigration and granted them land for intensive farming, but he refused to give the Chinese any say whatever in politics (and members of secret societies were to be executed on discovery). Politics was the concern of the Muslim Malays—who were used to governing, Brooke thought, and proto-gentlemen in their own right. So they became a professional class of minor officialdom, but were forbidden to dirty their hands in trade. The Iban, as long as they paid their "door tax" of one dollar per family per year, reported for war service on receipt of the Rajah's spear, curtailed their constant migrations in search of fresh land and otherwise kept the peace, were allowed to live exactly as they always had done.

Our path led past some scrappy huts on low stilts, over a wooden bridge, and up to the concrete block of the Rajang Hotel and two streets of Chinese shops. Glossy, tethered cockerels scratched about on the derelict land beyond the road margins. In the Rajang Hotel an excessively thin, bald, old Chinaman, suffering from a speech impediment, and looking as if his bones had been slightly crumpled, showed us to our rooms. We took spectre-free siestas and then patronised the local café to the right of the hotel entrance, a café run by a big, cuddly, Chinese mamma who reminded James of Ella Fitzgerald. After a reassuring and retarded meal of eggs and toast and coffee with condensed milk, we strolled further along the downstream path and found ourselves in the Malay Kampong. We admired the pretty houses and bungalows, each one set in its neat and tended garden; and James talked of the war in Vietnam and Cambodia, and, in particular, about one beleaguered regiment of hill-tribe boy-soldiers who, surrounded and unsupplied, had eaten all the Vietcong they could shoot. Told later by a visiting officer that the government could not afford to pay them the money they were owed, they had shot him too. James had seen the corpse lying face down on the ground. Part of the battledress and the backbone had been cut away, and the liver had gone.

As we walked back, a young Malay came running out of his garden gate towing a snake behind him. It was dead, quite thick, about sixteen feet long, and its head was stuck in a bamboo cage trap. The young man pulled it to the edge of a concrete platform above some steps leading down to a landing stage. He then, with some difficulty, heaved the body into the river. It must, we supposed, have been a small python.

We drank far too much beer with Ella Fitzgerald, and went to bed early.

The next morning I had a shave and a shower. I put on a white shirt, a clean pair of trousers, and James's Durham Cathedral School choirboy's tie. I persuaded the poet himself, as one well known to be Averse to Authority, to stay behind; and I walked up the hill to confront Immigration and The Police.

In my hand I carried my passport and a weighty piece of paper which I had just withdrawn from its protective wallet in my Bergen. Under duress, Christopher Butler, then Senior Proctor at Oxford, had equipped us with a talisman of medieval-looking splendour (and a document which pleased me profoundly every time I sneaked a glance at it). Above the scarlet impression of the Great Seal of the University it proclaimed

To whom it may concern

This is to certify that

JAMES FENTON, M.A. (Oxon), F.R.S.L.

and

REDMOND O'HANLON, M.A., M.Phil., D.Phil. (Oxon)

are personally known to me, and are members of the University of Oxford.

They are travelling in Borneo for Scientific purposes, and I would be grateful for any help and assistance you can give them.

The government offices were housed in a large modern building on the top road, and stood proudly behind their own extensive car park. There *are* only two miles of road in Kapit, a town surrounded by jungle and reachable only by river-launch or light aircraft, so each Toyota and Ford in the neat row, brought up from Sibu one at a time in a small cargo boat and lifted ashore by crane, represented a little victory for pleasure and status over common sense.

I found immigration and offered my passport to a young Iban behind the desk.

"I want permission to go up the Baleh to its headwaters and then to climb Mount Tiban," I said. "James Fenton and I wish to re-discover the Borneo rhinoceros."

"Do you indeed?" said the clerk, smiling. "I am afraid that that is impossible. Out of the question. It is too far for us to reach you if you are in trouble. It is very far, very far. It is expensive. It is dangerous. There are no maps. We will not allow it. The police will not allow it. So where else would you like to go?"

I placed the document in front of him. The paper stirred slightly in the air current from the ceiling fan. The red wax of the seal glowed in the sunlight filtering through the blinds. The clerk picked it up, read it, and disappeared into a back office.

In five minutes he returned.

"My name is Bidai," he said. "We will find you the best trackers in Kapit. The best boat crew there is. I will bring them to your hotel tonight."

Bidai arrived with two other educated Ibans from his own department, Siba and Edward.

"Bidai has persuaded our Tuai Rumah to come with you," said Siba, shaking our hands. "He is what you would call a Headman, a chief. He is much respected here, the Head of all the Iban of Kapit. He used to be a great soldier. He knows the rivers. You will travel in a canoe he made himself."

"What about the others?" said James. "We'll need more than one won't we?"

"Our Tuai Rumah Dana has picked two young men from our longhouse," said Edward. "Leon is very strong. Inghai is very small, and a good bow look-out. He can concentrate all day. You'll be in good hands. And we've fixed everything with the police. You must collect your passes tomorrow."

"Come on," said Bidai, "they're waiting in the café. You can talk; and then we'll all get drunk together. Leon speaks a little English, so you'll be all right. Come and buy us lots of beer."

Dana, forceful, intelligent, full of natural authority, had ear-lobes distended into hanging loops and was tattooed on his throat and hands. He wore a tee-shirt and long trousers; and so did Leon and Inghai, two young men who, I realised with secret disappointment, their ears the shape they were born with, their hands unmarked, would not have drawn a second glance on an Oxford street.

With lots of advice and translation and encouragement from the senior officers (First Class) of the Kapit Immigration Department,

Siba and Edward, we overcame the seemingly impossible difficulties of calculating a fair wage (we agreed to pay the government rate for crews taking officers to visit longhouses, plus a quarter for the extra risk); we worked out how many gallons of petrol we would need (600 dollars-worth); we made lists of stores to buy in Kapit: salt, rice, aginomoto, cooking oil, onions, ginger, candles, sugar, cigarettes, coffee, arak, and cartridges.

The night before we were due to leave, Leon called to take us to Dana's longhouse. He was becoming less shy and awkward and, when Bidai and Siba and Edward were not about, he was prepared to talk in English. As we left the hotel and walked up the hill he drew me aside.

"Redmon," he said, *sotto voce*, "I hopes you and Jams not go with hotel girls?"

"I haven't seen any hotel girls."

"They on top floor. Very naughties."

"Do you go with hotel girls?"

"No Redmon," said Leon, with great seriousness, "there is new diseases here. Your spear it rots. You go to hospital, they look at your spear, you take medicine. We have a word for this diseases. I not know it in English. We Iban, in our language, we call it *syphilis*."

The road wound up out of the town, past a small airstrip and a group of government houses and into secondary jungle. We turned off on to a footpath which curved along the sides of a series of small hills. I carried a kit-bag containing presents for Dana: two bottles of whisky, an outsize pipe made in London, a tin of Balkan Sobranie, and my cartridge belt. This last, an English, old, hand-sewn, worn, and desirable cartridge belt, I was parting with under protest ("But Redmond," James had said, "what possible use could it be now you've been disarmed? What do you mean—it's a *lucky* cartridge belt, you've shot *lots of pheasants* with it? Redmond, you are an Ignoble Savage.").

The jungle around us was secondary jungle, a re-growth of thick vegetation, of tangled young trees and bushes and creepers on ground that had been felled, burned and cleared for a season's crop of hill padi perhaps ten or fifteen years ago. Rounding a bend on the path, we found ourselves staring straight at a raven-sized bird with a deep chestnut-coloured back, a hooked beak, a red eye and a long black tail. It hopped off the branch of a small tree, flapped twice and floated, its wings outstretched, its legs hanging, across a small clearing and into dense bushes where it disappeared from view.

"What the hell was that, Leon?" I said.

"Bubut," said Leon. "He is a friend to the Iban. We leave him alone. He helps us grow padi. He eat all the insect."

When I looked up the Chestnut-raven-glider in Smythies, later, there was no possibility of mistaking such a forceful identity: it was a Common coucal, *Centropus sinesis*, a cuckoo that builds its own nest, a good, honest, "bulky ball of grass with the entrance at the side". In the coucal's case, however, it might have been wiser to put one's eggs in other people's incubation baskets, because

In Sabah the young of both this and the Lesser Coucal are used medicinally by natives and Chinese alike. When they locate a nest they keep a very close watch upon it until the chicks are hatched and then, a day or two later, they break the legs of the chicks. They believe that upon finding the chicks injured the parent birds forage for healing herbs which they half-digest and then regurgitate to use as a dressing on the limbs. The legs quickly heal and mend, and the goodness of the medicine is (they believe) retained in the blood of the chicks. The procedure may be repeated and often the chicks are hand fed with cooked rice for a few days before being collected and bottled whole in brandy or other spirit. The resulting liquid is used both internally and externally as a cure-all, especially for rheumatic complaints.

The track straightened and Dana's longhouse was revealed in front of us. Pressed into a small space between the conical hills, it was massive. There had obviously been no room to expand the settlement lengthways, so the longhouse had been split into two sections, two rows of continuous dwellings raised some fifteen feet from the ground on a mass of stilts and sharing a broad communal verandah, the doors of the individual rooms facing each other across it. Further up the hill and connected to the main longhouse by wooden steps was the Headman's house. It was two storeys high, roofed with corrugated iron and built with machine-made planking. Amongst the democratic, socially easy-going Iban whose chief's house is usually distinguished from the others solely by its central position in the line of dwellings, Dana's comparative palace was very special indeed.

But then Dana, I realise now, was no ordinary Iban. He must have been named after his famous ancestor, the great pirate and headhunter Orang Kaya Pamancha Dana, one of the few Iban (as Charles Brooke himself testifies in his memoir, *Ten Years in Sarawak*, 1866) who actually led Malays into battle rather than the other way about; Pamancha Dana came from a long line of leaders on the Saribas and was that Iban rarity, an hereditary chief. He specialised in raids into Dutch territory, taking his war fleets down the coast as far as Pontianak. But his most spectacular battle was a defensive action against the combined forces of James Brooke and the crew of Captain Keppel's HMS *Dido*, in June 1843. Armed with captured Dutch cannon, his mixed army of 500 Malays and 6,000 Ibans inflicted severe casualties on Brooke's expeditionary force from three "formidable-looking forts", wooden stockades at the junction of the Padeh and Layar rivers, before retreating into the jungle from the superior British firepower. James Brooke concluded a peace with Dana two years later and described their meeting in his journal: "The Orang Kaya Pamancha of Saribas is now with me—the dreaded and the brave, as he is termed by the natives. He is small, plain-looking and old, with his left arm disabled, and his body scarred with spear wounds. I do not dislike the look of him, and of all the chiefs of that river I believe he is the most honest, and steers his course straight enough."

Our Dana traced his own line of descent from Ibans who had settled in the lower Baleh (whence Charles Brooke had forced them to move down to Kapit); who in turn had migrated from the Kapuas river basin in Dutch Borneo, where they had moved from the Saribas. So perhaps it was indeed his ancestor who had once boasted that he would have James Brooke's head in a basket before the next padisowing.

One could believe so, anyway, looking at Dana's Chief-of-Chief's collection of cotton trousers and shorts and tee-shirts which lay in neat piles, on shelves from floor to ceiling, in a corner of his room. A few cheap modern chairs were scattered about, and magazine cutouts of the Queen and the Duke of Edinburgh adorned a patch of wall-planking.

Dana signed to us to sit on the floor. Dana's wife brought us mugs of tuak. I gave Dana the precious cargo in my kit-bag, which he put aside without a word. Siba and Edward and Inghai arrived, and about twenty men and women drifted in and sat down against the walls.

A dark red-brown, richly decorated Iban blanket was spread on the floor. On its far edge Dana placed six bundles, somethings of different sizes wrapped in old, worn, dirty cloth and tied tightly with rattan lashings which had frayed at their knots. Leon sat beside me and Siba beside James.

"We now make the bedara," said Leon. "It protect us from harms on our great journey. We make the spirits look after us."

Dana sat cross-legged on the blanket. Three pretty girls, his daughters, entered the main room from the kitchen at the back, wearing, over their dresses, from just above their hips to just below their breasts, close-stacked loops of rattan hung with polished, shining, clinking roundels of beaten silver. They bore trays loaded with small bowls, which they placed in three lines in front of Dana. Furthest from him, they set eight bowls of rice cakes, then eight bowls of puffed rice, then eight bowls of sticky rice; three larger bowls, containing, respectively, salt and rice, leaves to wrap around and chew with betel nut, and shredded tobacco, were positioned by his right hand.

Having returned to the kitchen and re-filled their trays the girls presented Dana with a small cup full of a mixture of tuak and beaten eggs; a small bowl of the same; a glass of tuak; one large bowl of eggs; one large bowl piled with bundles of puffed rice wrapped in banana leaf and with packets of sticky rice rolled up in palm leaves; and one empty plate.

Everyone watched as Dana picked up the small cup, got to his feet, walked out on to the verandah and tipped its contents through the planking to the ground below.

"For the spirits to drink," said Leon. "In case they are thirsties."

Dana sat down cross-legged, drained his glass of tuak without pausing for breath, leaned forward over the various dishes, and concentrated.

"He must not make mistake," whispered Leon. "One wrongs and the spirits will not like us. We will not go with you."

Very carefully, on the empty plate, Dana placed the tobacco, the betel leaves, the salt-and-rice, in the middle. Around the edge, slowly, he arranged the rice cakes, the sticky rice, the puffed rice.

Leon nudged me.

26

"Redmon, you watch," he hissed in my ear, "you and Jams must do it, too. Then we know if we all safe or not. You must get it right."

"Jesus, James, how are we going to remember?" I whispered.

"In my opinion, we are up shit creek in a barbed wire canoe," said James, "with no paddles."

Siba overheard, and grinned.

"Do not worry," he said, putting his hand on James's knee, "I will help you."

Reaching for the eggs, Dana balanced the first one, end up, in the middle. He lay the rest, on their sides, around the outer rim. Making spaces round the central egg he added, with a pause for deliberation between each move, the sticky rice wrapped in palm leaves, the puffed rice wrapped in banana leaves, and the little bowl of beaten egg and tuak.

From somewhere near the door, a white cockerel was then passed from hand to hand until it reached the man nearest to Dana. The bird, which each man held firmly round the folded-down wings, was in peak condition, each feather glossily in place, its comb deep red, its eye bright.

Dana stood up and the holder of the cockerel held the bird out to him. With a quick twitch of his right hand at the upper tail coverts Dana plucked a small feather.

"Waaaaark!" said the cockerel.

At the tip of the quill there was a small drop of blood. Dana placed the feather between his palms and squeezed them together; he then stroked it across Leon and Inghai's right hand, and ministered, likewise, to us.

Taking the cockerel (its legs and talons hung down limp and unprotesting) Dana described a circle with it over the offering-dish; and then over the heads of Leon and Inghai and us, repeating some kind of prayer as he did so.

The bird was sent back the way it had come and tethered to the door-post with a rattan loop round its leg. It stood quietly, its head tilted on one side and then on the other, blinking, watching the puffed rice piled, in plain view, at the top of the sacred plate.

Dana cleared his throat and began to talk in Iban in his wildly energetic, emphatic manner.

"He welcomes you," whispered Leon. "He say you have come far, from the country of our old Rajahs. And now we take you on a great journey to Bukit Batu Tiban, where we have never gone. But Dana he know of it. He says we will go there, because the spirits like you. He says you will not want to go to the very tops. Jams is very, very old, because he have no hair; but you are young. He says if you stay a long time you marry his daughter. He says you are both very strongs, and giants. But he says that we remember, long, long ago, before our peoples came to Borneo, that we, too, we all white and giants. We orang puteh."

Dana then briefly held up the whisky bottles.

"He thank you for whiskies. We all get drunk," said Leon.

He held up the pipe and tobacco.

"He say he keep it till he die."

He picked up the cartridge belt, lifted it above his head, showed it to all four corners of the room. He ran his fingers over the twenty-five, neatsfoot-oil-stained, twelve-bore pouches. He buckled it round his spare and muscled waist. It hung down in front, almost to his knees.

"He says he never sees such a belt before," said Leon, "not in all his life. It so beautifuls. It made in Inglang. It go hunting in Inglang, often. He can see it marked with many journeys, many huntings. It so beautifuls it belong to all of us. It bring all we Iban good lucks hunting the pig. Our Tuai Rumah, he say he not forget tonight, because now we have a new good lucks to add to our other good lucks. He tie it in cloth tomorrow. Then, Redmon, only the spirits can see inside."

Dana walked over to the verandah side of the room, undid the belt, and, reaching up, placed it in an inverted gong hanging from a rafter.

"He put it in the spirit-house," said Leon.

The wrapped bundles were next to go in, followed, very carefully, by the offering-dish.

Everybody clapped. The whisky was opened. The girls filled our glasses with tuak. We began to get drunk.

Later, we walked down to the main longhouse and repeated the whole process, with much help from Siba, on the bamboo-floored verandah outside the rooms owned by Leon and Inghai's families. James, as poet, made up the Inglang prayer that was demanded of us.

"We pray to the spirits of the jungle," he said, "for good success, good hunting, and a safe return."

Months later, it seemed, as we lay, full of tuak, on the springy, split-bamboos, James made another pronouncement. "Redmond," he said, "in my opinion, and I realise you may not agree, and that is perfectly okay, please yourself, I think it is high time we pinched a little of that sleep that ravels up the knitted sleeve of care."

"That's not right," I said.

"Want to bet?" said James.

We stumbled all the way back to Kapit.

FIVE

In the last Sea Dyak longhouse upstream on the Baleh river, Rumah Pengulu-Jimbun, were a great many skulls hanging in rattan nets from the cross-beams of the gallery roof. I inspected them carefully. The teeth had been worn almost uniformly flat, and there were no fillings, which was comforting. Each one was busily tenanted, not by brains, but by digger wasps. Too large to crawl in by the optic nerve holes behind the eye-sockets, the insects had made their entrances at the base of the crania, where the heads had been severed from their spinal columns.

"Very old," said Leon, our tracker and interpreter, who was good at guessing one's thoughts at such moments. "Maybe some belong Japanese."

"Come on—surely just a little head-hunting still goes on?" I asked. "Every now and then when no one is looking?"

"No, no—absolute no. But if," said Leon with one of his big brown grins, "if we find someone we don't like, not one bit, all alone in the jungle, then that's called murder; and that's quite different. And then it would be a waste not to take his head, wouldn't it?"

"But you took a lot of Japanese heads, didn't you?" I said, thinking of Tom Harrisson's ten-bob-a-nob campaign in the war.

"Every one of them, all of them," said Leon with great seriousness. "You ask the old men, you ask Dana. Just around that far bend in the river, by the rapids beyond the islands, one of the great battles in the Second World War took place. There were eight Japanese, all armed with guns, coming up in a boat they'd stolen from us. And we had two hundred warriors from here with their spears and blowpipes hidden on the left bank, and two hundred warriors from two different longhouses hidden on the right bank, and they killed all the Japanese. And so there were eight heads, but there were three chiefs, and so they fought because they couldn't divide them equally. You know about the Second World War?"

"Just a bit," I said.

"Well—one party of Japanese came to Borneo to take our padi. And one party stayed at home. And the Japanese were so cruel to the Iban that the English couldn't bear it. So they came to help us. But there weren't enough English to kill all the Japanese in both places, so they asked the Americans to help. So the Americans bombed the longhouses at Hiroshima and Nagasaki and the English helped us to take all the heads of all the Japanese in Borneo and that was the end of the Second World War."

"And a good thing too," I said.

An old man (old for Borneo), apparently blind, sitting in the shade on the split-bamboo floor, attacked by some disease which had destroyed the pigment in his cells and left him blotched with white, nodded.

At midday, waving goodbye to the chief and to the thirty or forty children and the thirty or forty dogs which had gathered on the bank, we climbed into our dugout canoe and set off upriver towards the interior, where neither Dana, nor Leon nor Inghai (our youngest tracker and our bow look-out) had ever been. For us, the unknown had begun at the coast, at the delta of the great river Rajang; for them, the unknown began now.

After about ten miles the hill-padi fields of Rumah Pengulu-Jimbun gave way to well-established secondary forest, ground whose vegetation had not been slashed and burned and cleared for a one-year's crop of rice for fifty years or so; and then the primeval jungle began. The river seemed to close in on us: the two-hundred-foot-high trees crowded down the slopes of the hills, almost to the water's edge, an apparently endless chaos of different species of tree, every kind of green, even under the uniform glare of a tropical sun; parasitic growths sprouted everywhere, ferns fanned out from every angle in the branches, creepers as thick as legs gripped each other and tangled down to the surface of the water, their tips twining down in the current like river-weed.

The river itself began to turn and twist, too, the banks behind us appearing to merge together into one vast and impenetrable thicket, shutting us in from behind just as the trees ahead stepped aside a meagre pace or two to let the river swirl down ahead. The outboard motor, manned by Leon and set on a special wooden frame at the stern of the canoe, pushed us past foaming little tributaries, islets, shingle banks strewn with huge rounded boulders, half-hidden coves scooped round by whirlpools. Way above the last of the logging camps whose bulldozed topsoil, falling into the water, turns the lower reaches of the rivers of Borneo brown, here the Baleh was clear, deep green from the reflection of the trees. We really were voyaging upriver—at first I thought it an optical illusion, but the canoe was actually climbing up a volume of water great enough to sustain an almost constant angle of ascent, even on the stretches of water between the jagged steps of the rapids.

Spits of land had formed wherever smaller streams joined the main flow, and here driftwood was piled, stacks of hardwood planed smooth by the rush of floodwater, flung together, bleached grey by the sun. We stopped by one such pile to hide a drum of petrol. A monitor lizard, reared up on its front legs, watched us for a moment with its dinosauric eyes and then scuttled away between the broken branches. A Brahminy kite, flying low enough for us to hear the rush of air through the primary feathers of its wings, circled overhead watching us, its flecked-brown belly white in the sun, before it soared away, mewing its shrill call like a buzzard.

Further up, the rapids began to become more numerous and more turbulent and, at each one, as Leon drove the canoe for the central cascade of the current at full power whilst Dana and Inghai, their back muscles bunched, poled the bow to the left or the right of each oncoming rock, heavy waves of water would crash over and into the boat. James, sitting opposite me on the duckboards in the centre of the canoe and facing upstream, was reading his way through Pat Rogers's new edition of the complete poems of Swift, a straw boater on his bald head, his white shirt buttoned at the neck and at the wrists.

"Some of this juvenilia is pretty feeble," James would mutter, displeased.

"Quite so. But—er—James?"

"Yes?"

"Rapid 583/2, Green Heave Strength six-out-of-ten, is approaching."

With a second or two to spare, James would shut his book, mark his place in it with a twig, slip it neatly under an edge of the tarpaulin, place his left buttock upon it, shut his eyes, get drenched, open his eyes, squeeze the water from his beard with his right hand, retrieve his book and carry on reading.

Every five hundred yards or so, a Lesser fish-eagle would regard us with its yellow eye, motionless at first, its grey feet clamped to a favourite branch overhanging the edge of the river, flying off only as we drew almost level, flapping gently just ahead of the canoe to the limit of its territory, and then doubling back. There were Grey-headed fish-eagles, too, larger and more sluggish, the base of their tails white rather than grey-brown. It was odd to be journeying like this, preceded by eagles.

The first real sight of the Borneo kingfishers was equally startling. Brighter than any illustration could ever be, apparently radiating blue and orange from its back and stomach all around itself into the background of green until it seemed to be a bird four times its size, its large bill translucent, carmine-red in the sun, the Black-capped kingfisher (in fact an eater of insects) was often so tame it never bothered to fly from us at all, but sat bobbing on its bough, *chick-chicking* loud and shrill, furious to be disturbed. The Stork-billed kingfisher, however, much bigger, its front end built like the nose-cone of a missile, always flew off, screaming as it went, the silky light blue of its rump disappearing fast and low upriver to a hiding-perch in some habitual tree.

A small heron, the Little green heron, slate-grey and furtive, skulked about the river margins, or the island shingle banks, or amongst the beached driftwood; and our own Common sandpiper, always solitary (except at dusk when we might see three or four come skimming past just above the water) seemed to like riding on drifting logs, hopping off to run about the mud or the shingle.

Looking at one, as small and brown, as agile and elegant and friendly as if I had been watching it in Poole Harbour, I thought of Beccari's record of one of its feeding habits: "When crocodiles lie thus with open jaws, small shore birds, especially waders of the sandpiper kind, which are always running about on the banks in search of food, enter the huge reptiles' mouths to capture any such small fry as may have sought refuge among the teeth or in the folds of the mucous membrane of the mouth or pharynx. Indeed, if I remember right, I have witnessed the thing myself; but now as I write I cannot feel quite sure that it was not one of many stories told me by my men."

James, his huge head laid back on the hump of our kit under the tarpaulin, was having one of his five-minute snoozes. The vein on his right temple was distended with blood, a sure sign that his cerebellum was awash with extra dissolved oxygen, and that some piece of programming, vital to the production of a future poem, was in progress.

"James!"

An eye opened.

"What is it?"

"Just this—if you *do* see a log floating *upriver*, let me know."

"Crocodiles?"

"Well, not the estuarine one that really goes for you. Not up here. But Tweedie and Harrison think we might see the freshwater Gharial. The fifteen-foot one with the five-foot snout and all those teeth."

"Really Redmond," said James, raising himself up on an elbow and looking about, "you're absurd. You live in the nineteenth century. Everything's changed, although you don't appear to notice. Nowadays you will have no difficulty whatever in recognising a crocodile. Everyone knows—they come with an outboard motor at the back and a Kenwood mixer at the front."

I sat back in the boat. When the temperature is 110° and the humidity 98 per cent, when you're soaking wet and rotting a bit in the crutch, then even weak jokes like that, in the worst possible taste, seem extraordinarily funny.

At five o'clock in the afternoon we entered a wider stretch of river where a tributary joined the main stream and a low ridge of shingle had formed down the centre of the water course. Dana decided to make camp.

"Good fishing. Very good," said Leon, looking at the swirling white water, the fallen trees and the eddies by the far bank.

We pulled the canoe well out of the water and tied its bow-rope high up the trunk of a tree, in case of floods in the night, and then stretched out on the sand for a rest. Butterflies began to gather. Hundreds of butterflies, flying at different heights and speeds, floating, flapping awkwardly in small bursts, gliding, fluttering like bats, winnowing, some flying fast and direct like a wren in trouble, made their way towards us and settled on our boots and trousers, clustered on our shirts, sucked the sweat from our arms. There were Whites, Yellows and Blues; Swallow-tails, black, banded or spotted with blue-greens; and, just outside the clustering circle of small butterflies, the magnificent species which Alfred Russel Wallace named after James Brooke, *Troides brookiana*, the Rajah Brooke's birdwing.

Sucking our clothes and skin with their thread-like proboscides at one end, the butterflies exuded a white goo over us from their anal vents at the other. Getting up, brushing them off as gently as possible, I walked away from my companion the mandatory few yards and took a pee myself. Whilst my patch of urine was still steaming slightly on the muddy sand, the males of Rajah Brooke's birdwing (the females, fully employed laying eggs in the jungle trees, are seldom seen) flew over and crowded down on it, elbowing each other with the joints on their legs, pushing and shoving to get at the liquid, the brilliant green feather-shaped marks on their black wings trembling slightly as they fed. I began, prematurely, to feel a part of things.

In fact, having run to the canoe to fetch the shock-proof, water-proof, more-or-less-everything-proof (but, sadly, fixed-lens) heavy-duty Fuji cameras, I began to feel, as I crawled on my stomach towards the pullulating insects, more than a passing pride in the quality of my offering. After all, some thirteen inches from my own nose and closing, was the very butterfly which Wallace described in 1855:

the Ornithoptera Brookeana, one of the most elegant species known. This beautiful creature has very long and pointed wings, almost resembling a sphinx moth in shape. It is deep velvety black, with a curved band of spots of a brilliant metallic-green colour extending across the wings from tip to tip, each spot being shaped exactly like a small triangular feather, and having very much the effect of a row of the Wing Coverts of the Mexican trojon laid upon black velvet. The only other marks are a broad neck-collar of vivid crimson, and a few delicate white touches on the outer margins of the hind wings. This species, which was then quite new and which I named after Sir James Brooke, was very rare. It was seen occasionally flying swiftly in the clearings, and now and then settling for an instant at puddles and muddy places, so that I only succeeded in capturing two or three specimens.

While photographing this butterfly (with a fixed wide-angle lens which I knew would produce a hopeless picture), which later proved to be very common all the way up the Baleh to its source, I felt the excitement that Wallace himself describes, on capturing its close cousin *Ornithoptera croesus*: "Fine specimens of the male are more

35

than seven inches across the wings, which are velvety black and fiery orange, the latter colour replacing the green of the allied species. The beauty and brilliancy of this insect are indescribable, and none but a naturalist can understand the intense excitement I experienced when I at length captured it . . . my heart began to beat violently, the blood rushed to my head, and I felt much more like fainting than I have done when in apprehension of immediate death. I had a headache the rest of the day, so great was the excitement produced by what will appear to most people a very inadequate cause."

I, too, had a headache for the rest of the day, but then perhaps it was the sun, or the mere thought of our fishing equipment. For after a burning swig all round from the arak rice-brandy five-gallon converted petrol-can, Dana, Leon and Inghai, drawing their parangs from their carved wooden scabbards, set off to cut down the saplings for our pole-beds; and I decided it was time that James and I taught them how to fish to maximum effect, like Englishmen. But first a little practice would be necessary.

Withdrawing quietly behind a massive jumble of boulders, well out of sight, I unpacked our precious cargo. Two new extendable rods, the toughest in town. A hundred yards of heavy line. A heavy bag of assorted lead weights. A termite's nest of swivels. A thornbush of hooks. Fifty different spinners, their spoons flashing in the sun, all shapes and all sizes for every kind of fish in every sort of inland water.

"The trouble is," said James, flicking a rod handle and watching the sections telescope out into the blue beyond, "my elder brother was the fisherman. That was his thing, you see, he filled that role. So I had to pretend it was a bore; and I never learned."

"What? You never fished?"

"No. Never. What about you?"

"Well, *my* elder brother went fishing."

"So you can't either?"

"Not exactly. Not with a rod. I used to go mackerel fishing with a line. All over the place."

"Mackerel fishing! Now you tell me!" said James, looking really quite agitated and frightening a bright orange damsel-fly off his hat. "Still," he said, calming down, "if *they* could do it it can't be that diffy, can it?"

"Of course not—you just stick the spinner and swivels and weights on that end and swing it through the air."

The heat was unbearable. The fiddling was insupportable. The gut

36

got tangled; the hooks stuck in our fingers; the knot diagram would have given Baden-Powell a blood clot in the brain. We did it all and forgot the nasty little weights. But eventually we were ready to kill fish.

"The SAS say it's simpler to stick in a hand-grenade."

"They're right," said James.

"But the Major said all you had to do was hang your dick in the river and pull it out with fish on it."

"Why don't you stick your dick in the river?" said James.

Standing firm and straight, James cast the spinner into the river. It landed in the water straight down at the end of the rod. Clunk. James pulled. The line snapped. We went through the whole nasty rigmarole again, with fresh swivels, weights and spinner.

"Try again. Throw it a little further."

James reached right back and then swung the rod forwards and sideways as if he was axeing a tree.

At that very moment, it seemed, the Borneo banded hornet, *Vesta tropica*, sunk its sting into my right buttock.

"Jesus!" I said.

It was huge and jointed, this hornet, flashing red and silver in the sun.

"You are hooked up," said James, matter-of-factly. "You have a spinner in your bum."

There was a weird, gurgling, jungle-sound behind us. Dana, Leon and Inghai were leaning against the boulders. The Iban, when they decide that something is really funny, and know that they are going to laugh for a long time, lie down first.

Dana, Leon and Inghai lay down.

"You should try it with harpoon!" shrieked Leon, helpless.

With great ceremony we presented our rods to Dana and Leon and a compensatory extra helping of weights and spinners to little Inghai. And with equal aplomb, the Iban took the useless gifts into care, wrapped them in cloth, and placed them in the bottom of the canoe.

Our beds had been expertly set up: two poles run through the specially-designed tubes of the SAS tarpaulins to form a stretcher, itself supported on a rectangular frame, a four-poster, lashed together with rattan strips and awaiting only a mosquito net and a cover. Tying the net and the canvas roof to the surrounding trees with parachute cord, a small bed-length of insect-free security emerged in the jungle. Campaign-proved, everything fitted, tied together, overlapped, held fast.

Dana and Leon had almost finished building their own shelter. Having constructed a platform of poles about two feet off the jungle floor, they were laying a lattice-work of branches to make a sloping roof. Inghai returned from the hillside with bundles of enormous palm leaves, and the structure was complete. Lying inside on a leaf-bed, one's feet towards the four-foot opening overlooking the river, the roof coming down at a bright green angle tight above one's head, it seemed the childhood tree-house *par excellence*.

Dana then began to build his own little house. Six-foot tall, two-feet square, with a conventional triangular roof and a small platform halfway up, its use was not apparent. For the spirits? For heads that might saunter by?

"For fish," said Leon, "for smoking fish. Now we show you how to fish like the Iban."

Taking their wooden harpoons from the canoe, Leon and Inghai dived into the river; and disappeared completely, like a pair of Great crested grebe. A full forty seconds later they bobbed up again, right over on the far bank. Leon stood up and held an enormous fish above his head, harpooned through the flank. Inghai, as befitted his size, held up a tiddler. Much yelling in Iban took place. Dana, evidently stung into action, took a large weighted net out of the canoe, a *jala*, and made his way upstream to the shingle bank. Swinging it back and forth in both hands, swaying slightly, he cast it out; a slowly spinning circle of white mesh settled on the water, and sank. Jumping in, scrabbling about to collect the bottom ends of the net, Dana finally scooped it all up again, together with three catfish. They looked at us lugubriously, an immensely long whisker or barbel, their feelers, drooping down from either side of their mouths. Dana detached them with the greatest care, avoiding their dorsal and pectoral spines which, presumably, were poisonous, and tossed them up the shingle.

Leon and Inghai returned with six fish, all of the same species, *Sebarau*, handsome, streamlined, and, unlike the smooth and mucus-covered catfish, armoured with large silver scales and adorned with a bold black bar down each side.

Inghai collected driftwood and made two fires, one on the beach and the other at the base of the smoking-house. Leon gutted the fish, cut them into sections, placed some in a salting tin, some on the smoking-rack, and some in a water-filled cooking pot. Two ancient cauldrons, slung from a high wooden frame, bubbled over the fire: one full of fish pieces and one full of sticky rice. Dana, having set a larger net part-across the current, supported by ropes to an overhanging branch and by white polystyrene floats, returned for supper.

Dusk came suddenly, and, equally suddenly, Eared nightjars appeared, hawking insects, stooping and turning in their haphazard, bat-like way, along the tops of the trees above the river banks, seeming half-transparent and weightless in their ghostly agility, like falcons weirdly deprived of their power and strike and push. And they were whistling to each other.

After about ten minutes, they vanished. Which was just as well, because it had dawned on me that the fish and rice in my mess-tin would need all the attention I could give it. The sebarau was tasteless, which did not matter, and full of bones, which did. It was like a hair-brush caked in lard. James had made the same discovery.

"Redmond, don't worry," he whispered, "if you need a tracheotomy I have a biro-tube in my baggage."

It was time to go to bed. We washed our mess-tins in the river, kicked out the fire on the beach, and stoked up the smoking-house fire with more wet logs. Slinging my soaking clothes from a tree with parachute cord, I rubbed myself down with a wet towel and, naked, opened my Bergen to pull out my set of dry kit for the night. Every nook and cranny in the bag was alive with inch-long ants. Deciding that anything so huge must be the Elephant ant, and not the Fire ant, which packs a sting like a wasp, I brushed the first wave off my y-fronts. Glancing up, I was astonished to see my wet clothes swarming with ants, too; a procession of dark ants poured down one side of the rope and up the other, and, all over my wet trousers, hundreds of different moths were feeding. Darkness seemed to rise from the leafy mush of the forest floor; and I rummaged quickly in the outside Bergen pocket for my army torch. As my fingers closed on it, everyone else's little fingers seemed to close on my arm. I drew it out fast and switched on: Elephant ants, this time with massive pincers, were suspended from hand to elbow. The soldiers had arrived. I flicked them off, gratified to hear yelps from James's basha as I did so. It was good to know they also went for poets.

Slipping under the mosquito net, I fastened myself into the dark-green camouflage SAS tube. It seemed luxuriously comfortable. You had to sleep straight out like a rifle; but the ants, swarming along the poles, rearing up on their back legs to look for an entry, and the mosquitoes, whining and singing outside the various tunes of their species in black shifting clouds, could not get in.

"Eeeeeee—ai—yack yack yack yack yack!" Something screamed in my ear, with brain-shredding force. And then everyone joined in.

"Eeeeeee—ai—yack yack yack yack yack te yooo!" answered every other giant male cicada, maniacally vibrating the tymbals, drumskin membranes in their cavity amplifiers, the megaphones built into their bodies.

"Shut up!" I shouted.

"Wah Wah Wah Wah Wah!" said four thousand frogs.

"Stop it at once!" yelled James.

"Clatter clitter clatter" went our mess-tins over the shingle, being nosed clean by three shrews.

The Iban laughed. The river grew louder in the darkness. Something hooted. Something screamed in earnest further off. Something shuffled and snuffled around the discarded rice and fish bits flung in a bush from our plates. A porcupine? A civet? A ground squirrel? The long-tailed giant rat? Why not a Clouded leopard? Or, the only really dangerous mammal in Borneo, the long-clawed, short-tempered Sun bear?

I switched off the torch and tried to sleep. But it was no good. The decibel-level was way over the limit allowed in discotheques. And, besides, the fire-flies kept flicking their own torches on and off; and some kind of phosphorescent fungus glowed in the dark like a forty-watt bulb.

I switched on again, clipped the right-angled torch on to my shirt, and settled down for a peaceful bedtime read with Hose and McDougall. Discussing the wars of the Kayan, Hose tells us that:

> If the defending party should come upon the enemy struggling against a rapid, and especially if the enemy is in difficulties through the upsetting of some of their boats, or in any other way, they may fall upon them in the open bed of the river, and then ensues the comparatively rare event, a stand-up fight in the open. This resolves itself in the main into hand-to-hand duels between pairs of combatants, as in the heroic age. The

warriors select their opponents and approach warily; they call upon one another by name, hurling taunts and swaggering boastfully in the heroic style. Each abuses the other's parents, and threatens to use his opponent's skin as a war-coat, or his scrotum as a tobacco-pouch, to take his head and to use his hair as an ornament for a *parang*-handle; or doubt as to the opponent's sex may be insinuated. While this exchange of compliments goes on, the warriors are manoeuvring for favourable positions; each crouches, thrusting forward his left leg, covering himself as completely as possible with his long shield, and dodging to and fro continually. The short javelins and spears are first hurled, and skilfully parried with spear and shield. When a man has expended his stock of javelins and has hurled his spear, he closes in with his *parang*. His enemy seeks to receive the blow of the *parang* on his shield in such a way that the point, entering the wood, may be held fast by it. Feinting and dodging are practised; one man thrusts out his left leg to tempt the other to strike as it and to expose his head in doing so. If one succeeds in catching his enemy's *parang* in his shield, he throws down the shield and dashes upon his now weaponless foe, who takes to his heels, throwing away his shield and relying merely on his swiftness of foot. When one of a pair of combatants is struck down, the other springs upon him and, seizing the long hair of the scalp and yelling in triumph, severs the neck with one or two blows of the *parang*.

It was definitely time to sleep.

At dawn the jungle was half-obscured in a heavy morning mist; and through the cloudy layers of rising moisture came the whooping call, the owl-like, clear, ringing hoot of the female Borneo gibbon.

Replacing the dry socks, pants, trousers and shirt inside two plastic bags inside the damp Bergen, tying them tightly to keep out the ants, I shook the wet clothes. A double-barrelled charge of insects propelled itself from inside my trouser-legs. I groomed my pants free of visible bugs, covered myself in SAS anti-fungus powder until my erogenous zone looked like meat chunks rolled in flour, ready for the heat, and forced my way into clammy battle-dress for the day. It was a nasty five o'clock start; but in half an hour the mist would be gone, the sun merciless, and the river-water soaking one anyway.

Every bush seemed to hold an unseen bird, all in full throat. There were blackbird and thrush, nightingale and warbler-like notes from every side, but more urgent and powerful and relentless, the fortissimo calls of babblers and trillers and bulbuls.

After a breakfast of fish and rice, we re-packed the dugout and set off upriver. The gibbons, having proclaimed the boundaries of their territories, ceased calling. The world changed colour from a dark watery blue to mauve to sepia to pink and then the sun rose, extraordinarily fast.

Inghai put on his peaked cap to shield his eyes from the sun as he sat on the bow and scanned the turbulent water ahead for rocks and logs; Dana, in chiefly style, wore his round hat, as large and intricately patterned as a gaming table; and Leon, proudly switching his outboard to full power, wore a mutant hybrid of pork-pie and homberg. James adjusted his boater, stretched out his legs on his half of the duckboards, and addressed himself to Swift.

Something large and flappy was crossing the river in front of us. Was it a bird disguised as a leaf-skeleton? Was it a day-flying bat disguised as a hair-net? Or was a lattice of tropical worms in transit across my retina? Very slowly, unconcerned, the something made its floating and dipping, floating and dipping, indecisive flight right over the boat: it was an odd idea indeed, *Hestia idea*, a butterfly with grey and white wings like transparent gauze, highly poisonous, and safe from predators. In one of the richest of tropical rain forests, in a natural zone which actually contains more kinds of butterflies and moths than all other habitats of the world put together, it was ridiculously pleasing to have identified just one more species, even if, as I eventually had to admit to James, it was the most immediately obvious of them all.

James, momentarily, re-directed his critical gaze from Swift's sometimes-defective scansion, and fixed it upon the surrounding jungle. With AI vision in both eyes which are set so far apart that he does, in this one respect, resemble a hammer-head shark, he announced, in a statement which later became formulaic and, for the Iban (and, well, just a little, for me) the incantation of a shaman of immeasurable age and wisdom summoning the spirits of the forest to dance before him: "Redmond, I am about to see something *marvellous*."

The canoe swung into the next bend and there, majestically perched upon a dead branch across an inlet, was a Crested serpent eagle.

"How's that?" said James.

The eagle was thick-set, black and brown and grey, his stomach lightly freckled, his head plumed flat. James was sitting up, boatered, bearded-black, his shirt dazzling white. James looked at the eagle. The eagle looked at James. The eagle, deciding that it was too early in the morning to hallucinate, flapped off into the jungle, puzzled.

Gradually, the rapids became more frequent, more difficult to scale. Leon would align the boat carefully in the deep pools beneath each one, open up to full throttle on a straight run, shut off the engine, cock the propeller well up out of the water as we hit the first curve of white foam, grab his pole as Inghai and Dana snatched up theirs, and then all three would punt the canoe up, in wild rhythm with each other.

They were lean, fit, strong with a lifetime of unremitting exercise, their muscles flexing and bunching, etched out as clearly as Jan van Calcar's illustrations to *De humani corporis fabrica*. But we were about to discover the one disadvantage in their fondly mistaken idea of ourselves, the present misconception in the ancient myth of their oral tradition, that the ancestors of their race had been white, and giants, as strong and courageous, as all-powerful as we, too, must be.

The solid tree-trunk keel of the hollowed-out canoe began to thud against the boulders beneath the cascades of water, lightly at first, and then with alarming violence as the day wore on. We had to jump out beneath each rapid, take the long bow-rope, walk up the stones strewn down beside the fall, wade into the deep current above and pull, guiding the bow up. The water pushed irregularly at our waist and knees, sometimes embracing us like a succubus might (after a year in prison), sometimes trying a flowing rugby tackle, sometimes holding our ankles in a hydrolastic gin-trap, but never entirely friendly. With nothing but locked spines and clamped cartilages we leant back against the great flow of water on its way to the South China Sea, against the forward pull of the rope; itself tugging and slackening as the poled boat broke free or stuck fast.

Just in time, by a deep pool, in a harbour formed by two massive fallen hardwoods, Dana ruled that it was noon and we were hungry. The boat was tied up, we collapsed, and Leon went fishing.

Spreading our wet clothes out on the burning hot boulders, James and I took a swim and a wash. The clear shallows were speckled with little fish, darting shoals of orange and silver, weaving flocks of black and red; there were dull-coloured tiddlers, minnow-like, and bright fish with streamers, their small fins fanning in the current; they gathered round our feet, fixed our toes with their tiny eyes, chased whirling flecks of soap in the current.

Dana, intrigued by medicated Vosene, shampooed his glossy black hair and then rinsed it by swimming very fast across the pool under-water, a moving V of ripples on the surface marking his passage through the spins and eddies. Wading ashore, even his dark-blue tattoos glistened in the sun. Covered in circles and rosettes, whorls and lines (soot from a cooking pot, mixed with sweetened water, and punched into the skin with a bamboo stick and small hammer) the large tattoo on his throat (the most painful of all to suffer, and the most likely to produce septicaemia) testified to his immediate courage; on his thighs an intricate pattern of stylised Rhinoceros hornbill heads bespoke his chiefly status; and on the top joints of his fingers a series of dots and cross-hatchings suggested that he had taken heads in battle, probably from the bodies of invading Indonesian soldiers killed in the 1962-66 confrontation by the SAS, with whom he had sometimes served as a tracker. Dignified, intelligent, full of natural authority, at forty an old man in the eyes of his tribe, he was the law-giver and judge of conduct, the arbiter of when to plant and when to harvest the padi, and, perhaps most important of all, the chief augurer to his people, the interpreter of the messengers of the gods, the birds.

He regarded us with protective amusement. We were like the white men he had met in the war, Leon had informed us in hushed tones; we had stayed in his longhouse and behaved like guests he could trust, not offending against custom, well-mannered. James and I, in turn, decided that Tuai Rumah Dana, Lord of the House, a Beowulf, or, more accurately, a warrior-king out of Homer, was a great improvement on all our previous headmasters, deans and wardens.

Leon surfaced by the far bank of the river, half-obscured by the roots of a giant tree which twisted into the water, but obviously excited, ferociously excited. He was yelling wildly in Iban to Dana and Inghai, "Labi-labi!" holding his harpoon cord with both hands; and, to us, "Fish! Round fish! Big round fish!"

Dana and Inghai leapt into the dugout and put off fast across the current. It seemed a lot of fuss about a fish, however big and round.

Dana cut two lengths of our parachute cord, one for himself and one for Inghai and, tying the boat to a branch, plunged in. Something thrashed and splashed, churning up the water between the three of them. Lowering the cord, knotted into a noose, Dana pulled it tight, secured it to the stern of the dugout; and then all three paddled back, towing something. The boat beached, they hauled on the parachute cord. Gradually, a shiny olive dome broke surface, almost round, and about three feet across. Two pairs of webbed, thick claws were thrusting against the water, front and back. Pulling it ashore in reverse, the Iban cut two holes at the rear of its carapace and threaded a lead of rattan through each slit. It was a large Mud turtle, *Trionyx cartilagineus*, one of whose specific characteristics, described by a so-called closet-naturalist in the nineteenth-century British Museum from trophies in the collection, had been, as Wallace liked to point out, these very same restraining holes at the back of the shell.

Left alone for a moment, the turtle's head began to emerge from a close-fitting sleeve, from folds of telescopic muscle. It had a flexible snout for a nose, a leathery green trunk; and a sad, watery eye. Dana's parang came down with great violence, missing the head, glancing off the cartilaginous armour, bucking the turtle, throwing up water and pebbles. The head retracted. Dana crouched, waiting. Some ten minutes later, the turtle once more began to look cautiously for its escape. Out came the head, inch by inch. With one blow, Dana severed the neck. The head rolled, quizzically, a little way across the sand.

After a lunch of rice and sebarau, Dana and Leon heaved the turtle on to its back, slit open its white belly, and threw its guts to the fish. The meat was cut into strips, salted, and stowed away in a basket on the boat. The empty shell, the blood drying, we left on the shingle.

The river twisted and turned and grew narrower and the great creepers, tumbling down in profusion from two hundred feet above our heads, edged closer. Every now and then we would pass a tangle of river-rubbish, leaves and sticks and dead ferns, seemingly caught in the lianas by floodwater some forty feet above the present water-level. So why did the high banks not show more sign of recent devastation? Idly watching one such clump as Leon arced the boat close to the bank before making a run up a rapid, we solved the mystery. A dumpy bird, thrush-sized, its blue and yellow beak framed by whiskers, black on its back, scarlet on its stomach, popped out of a side opening: the suspended bunches of debris were the nests of the Black-and-red broadbill.

The rapids and cascades became more frequent. We had to jump out into the river more often, sometimes to our waists, sometimes to our armpits, guiding the dugout into a side channel away from the main crash of the water through the central rocks, pushing it up the shallows.

"Saytu, dua, tiga—bata!" sang Dana, which even we could reconstruct as one, two, three, and push.

The Iban gripped the round, algae-covered stones on the river-bed easily with their muscled, calloused, spatulate toes. Our boots slipped into crevices, slithered away in the current, threatened to break off a leg at the ankle or the knee. It was only really possible to push hard when the boat was still, stuck fast, and then Headmaster Dana would shout "Badas!" "Well done!" But the most welcome cry became "Npan! Npan!", an invitation to get back in, quick.

Crossing one such deep pool, collapsed in the boat, the engine re-started, we found ourselves staring at a gigantic Bearded pig sitting quietly on his haunches on the bank. Completely white, an old and lonely male, he looked at us with his piggy eyes. Dana, throwing his pole into the boat, snatched up his shotgun; Leon, abandoning the rudder, followed suit. Inghai shouted a warning, the canoe veered sideways into the current, the shotguns were discarded, the boat re-aligned, and the pig, no longer curious, ambled off into the jungle, his enormous testicles swaying along behind him.

We entered a wide reach of foaming water. The choppy waves, snatching this way and that, had ripped caves of soil out of the banks, leaving hundreds of yards of overhang on either side. There was an ominous noise of arguing currents ahead. The rapids-preamble, the white water, the moving whirlpools, the noise ahead, was longer and louder than it ought to have been.

With the canoe pitching feverishly, we rounded a sweeping bend; and the reason for the agitated river, the unaccustomed roar, became obvious. The Green Heave ahead was very much higher than any we had met. There was a waterfall to the left of the river-course, a huge surging of water over a ledge, with the way to the right blocked by thrown-up trees, piles of roots dislodged upstream, torn out in floods, and tossed aside here against a line of rocks. There was, however, one small channel through, a shallow rapid, dangerously close to the main rush of water, but negotiable, separated from the torrent by three huge boulders.

Keeping well clear of the great whirlpool beneath the waterfall, Leon, guided between rocks by Inghai's semaphore-like gestures, brought the boat to the base of this normal-size rapid. Dana, James and I made our way carefully up with the bow-rope, whilst Leon and Inghai held the dugout steady.

Dana held the lead position on the rope; I stood behind him and James behind me. We pulled, Leon and Inghai pushed. The boat moved up and forward some fifteen feet and then stuck. Leon and Inghai walked up the rapid, kneeling, hunching and shoving, rolling small rocks aside to clear a channel. We waited on the lip of the rock above, pulling on the rope to keep the longboat straight, to stop it rolling sideways, tiring in the push of water round our waists. At last Leon and Inghai were ready. But the channel they had had to make was a little to our right as we looked down at them, a little to their left, a little closer to the waterfall. To pull straight we must move to our right. Dana pointed to our new positions.

It was only a stride or two. But the level of the river-bed suddenly dipped, long since scooped away by the pull of the main current. James lost his footing, and, trying to save himself, let go of the rope. I stepped back and across to catch him, the rope bound round my left wrist, snatching his left hand in my right. His legs thudded into mine, tangled, and then swung free, into the current, weightless, as if a part of him had been knocked into outer space. His hat came off, hurtled past his shoes, spun in an eddy, and disappeared over the lip of the fall.

His fingers were very white; and slippery. He bites his fingernails; and they could not dig into my palm. He simply looked surprised; his head seemed a long way from me. He was feeling underwater with his free arm, impossibly trying to grip a boulder with his other hand, to get a purchase on a smooth and slimy rock, a rock polished smooth, for centuries, by perpetual tons of rolling water.

His fingers bent straighter, slowly edging out of mine, for hour upon hour, or so it felt, but it must have been in seconds. His arm rigid, his fingertips squeezed out of my fist. He turned in the current, spread-eagled. Still turning, but much faster, he was sucked under; his right ankle and shoe were bizarrely visible above the surface; he was lifted slightly, a bundle of clothes, of no discernible shape, and then he was gone.

"Boat! Boat!" shouted Dana, dropping the rope, bounding down the rocks of the side rapid, crouched, using his arms like a baboon.

"Hold the boat! Hold the boat!" yelled Leon.

James's bald head, white and fragile as an owl's egg, was sweeping round in the whirlpool below, spinning, bobbing up and down in the foaming water, each orbit of the current carrying him within inches of the black rocks at its edge.

Leon jumped into the boat, clambered on to the raised outboard-motor frame, squatted, and then, with a long, yodelling cry, launched himself in a great curving leap into the centre of the maelstrom. He disappeared, surfaced, shook his head, spotted James, dived again, and caught him. Inghai, too, was in the water, but, closing with them for a moment, he faltered, was overwhelmed, and swept downstream. Leon, holding on to James, made a circuit of the whirlpool until, reaching the exit current, he thrust out like a turtle and they followed Inghai downriver, edging, yard by yard, towards the bank.

Obeying Dana's every sign, I helped him coax the boat on to a strip of shingle beneath the dam of logs. James, when we walked down to him, was sitting on a boulder. Leon sat beside him, an arm around his shoulders.

"You be all right soon, my friend," said Leon "you be all right soon, my very best friend. Soon you be so happy."

James, bedraggled, looking very sick, his white lips an open O in his black beard, was hyper-ventilating dangerously, taking great rhythmic draughts of oxygen, his body shaking.

"You be okay," said Leon. "I not let you die my old friend."

Just then little Inghai appeared, beaming with pride, holding aloft one very wet straw boater.

"I save hat!" said Inghai, "Jams! Jams! I save hat!"

James looked up, smiled, and so stopped his terrible spasms of breathing. He really was going to be all right.

Suddenly, it all seemed funny, hilariously funny. "Inghai saved his hat!" We laughed and laughed, rolling about on the shingle. "Inghai saved his hat! Ingy-pingy saved his hat!" It was, I am ashamed to say, the first (and I hope it will be the last) fit of genuine medically-certifiable hysterics which I have ever had.

Dana, looking at James, decided that we would camp where we were. Finding a level plateau way above flood level on the bank behind us, the pole hut and the pole beds were soon built. I had a soap and a swim, re-covered myself in SAS super-strength insect repellent and silky crutch powder, re-filled our water bottles from the river and dosed each one with water-purifying pills, took a handful of vitamin pills myself, forced James and the Iban to take their daily measure, too, and then settled down against a boulder with my pipe (to further discourage mosquitoes), a mess-mug full of arak, and the third edition of Smythies's *The Birds of Borneo*.

James, covered in butterflies, was reading *Les Misérables* and looking a little miserable himself.

"How are you feeling?"

"Not too good, Redmond. I get these palpitations at the best of times. I've had attacks ever since Oxford. I take some special pills for it but they're really not much help. In fact the only cure is to rest a bit and then be violently sick as soon as possible."

"Can I do anything?"

"No," said James, pulling on his umpteenth cigarette and concentrating on Victor Hugo.

He was, I decided, an even braver old wreck than I had imagined. Looking fondly at his great bald head I was really fairly pleased with Leon for helping the future of English literature; for preventing the disarrangement of all those brain cells; for denying all those thousands of brightly-coloured little fish in the shallows the chance to nibble at torn fragments of cerebellar tissue, to injest synapses across which had once run electrical impulses carrying stored memories of a detailed knowledge of literature in Greek and Latin, in German and French, in Spanish and Italian. But all the same, I wondered, what would we do if an accident befell us in the far interior, weeks away from any hospital, beyond the source of the Baleh, marching through the jungle towards the Tiban range and well away, even, from the stores in the boat?

Dana took his single-barrelled shotgun, held together with wire and stips of rattan, and set off to find a wild pig. Leon and Inghai went fishing with their harpoons. My Balkan Sobranie tobacco, as ninety-per-cent humid as everything else, tasted as rich and wet as a good gravy, and the more arak I had, the less like fermented elasto-plast it became. And it actually made one see things.

A long white strip of silk chiffon detached itself from the tumul-tuous green tumble of trees and creepers on the opposite bank and undulated, as slowly as a lamprey in a lake, diagonally downstream. It was a very feminine apparition, redolent of everything I was begin-ning to miss, of silky rustles, lacy white knickers, of mysteriously intricate suspenders, of long, soft, white silk stockings dropped beside the bed. I looked at the arak with increased respect, and took some more.

A question framed itself, with great deliberation. What if, just supposing for a moment, it was not a suspender belt, but a butterfly? There were weirder things in the air in Borneo than suspender belts, after all. There was, for instance, and I planned to see it near Mount Tiban, an owl, *Glaucidium borneense*, "about the size of one's thumb", as Hose described it, which calls poop-te-poop-poop; "and also a tiny hawk, *Microhierax*, which lays a large white egg about as big as itself". Birds of the high montane moss forests they "settle on the dead trees; and as these are of a notable height, they look like insects, being in fact very much smaller than some of the large butterflies".

In fact—perhaps it was a bird? Maybe I could identify it in Smythies without leaving my increasingly comfortable boulder to rummage for the small library in my Bergen, Home of the Ant? There it was—unmistakable, the male Paradise flycatcher, trailing two white tail feathers, each eighteen inches long. Its call is *"auk auk* very like that of a frog (Banks). One of the loudest calls in the forest— both sexes call (Harrisson)." So it was a bird that looked like a butterfly, flew like a suspender belt, and sang like a frog. I fell into a deep sleep.

Leon woke me up for supper, handing me a mess-tin of sebarau and rice. Dana returned, his legs running with blood.

"What the hell's happened to him, Leon?"

"It's nothing! That's—how you say it? Leeches?"

Dana washed his legs in the river and joined us round Inghai's fire. He handed me a couple of cartridges, gesticulating angrily. The fulminite caps had been banged in by the firing pin, but the tube was still crimped, the main charge of powder unexploded. I laid them gingerly under a rock.

"They must have got wet."

"No," said Leon. "Dana says Malay cartridges, Chinese cartridges, no good. English cartridges always go off, boom! He creep up on two pigs. Click. Nothing at all. He put in another. Click. The pigs hear him. Foof. They run away. So no babi. No roast babi in a pot. Only fishes stew."

"Leon," I said, "why did you cry like that, when you saved James's life?"

"Well," said Leon, shuffling his bare feet on the sand, "we Christians like you, of course, but, all the same, we respect the river. The river like Jams. The river take Jams away. So we say sorries to the river, because we take him back again."

James was picking at his bony fish in the mess-tin, pushing his rice aside.

"Excuse me," he said, got up, lurched a little, and was horribly sick into a bush.

"Now you better, my best friend," said Leon, "now I give you more rices. Makai! Eat up! Makai, Jams!"

The sky grew black suddenly. There was an odd breeze. Everyone—insects, monkeys, birds, frogs—stopped making a noise. Dana, Leon and Inghai ran to the dugout, dragged it high up the shingle and re-tied it, bow and stern, with long ropes leading to trees on the high bank. Huge globules of water began to fall, splashing star-burst patterns on the dry hot rocks along the shore. We made for the bashas, changed fast, and slipped inside. Rain splattered on the tree canopy two hundred feet above, a whispery noise growing duller and increasing in volume to a low drumming. Drops hit our canvas awnings and bounced off; a fine spray came sideways through the mosquito net. A wind arrived; and we heard the first tree start its long crashing fall far off in the forest. Thunder rumbled nearer, and, every few seconds, the trunks of the trees immediately in view through the triangular gap at the foot of the basha were bright with lightning flashes, reflected power from balls and sheets and zig-zags of light, energy that lit the clumps of lichen on the bark with startling clarity, that picked out the tendrils of fungus and the stalks of spore-bodies like heads of unkempt hair.

I fell asleep and I dreamed of James's sister Chotty. She was coming at me with a particular knife she uses to make her beef stews, her pheasant pies. "It's quite all right," she said. "It doesn't matter now that he's drowned. There's no need to apologise. I don't want to hear your explanations."

• SEVEN •

In the morning, the world was soaked, the mist was thick, and the river had risen five or six feet. After a breakfast of rice and fish, James and I walked ahead up the steeply sloping bank and Dana and Leon and Inghai easily brought the boat up the now-deeper side rapid. The water was full of broken branches, old logs which had broken free from their previous snags, ferns, lengths of creeper, and mud. A dead green bird like a parakeet, perhaps a Green broadbill, floated past.

Dana confined James to the boat, or else put us ashore beneath a rapid, making us walk up and round it and picking us up beside the pools above; but in any case the temporary change in water-level made the going easier, submerging some cataracts altogether, filling channels through others. We had almost grown accustomed to the kingfishers, the herons, the fish-eagles that escorted us ahead. But there was one bird that always puzzled me, a new concept in eagles, occasionally wheeling over us, screaming its shrill cry, repeating it again and again. Sometimes it made this call and it was black; sometimes it made the same call and it was white, and barred-brown under the wings. One of them might have been Blyth's Hawk eagle, but for the cry. Probably, as Smythies told us, it was the Changeable hawk eagle, an odd species in which, in part-defiance of Darwin's rules for the mechanism of sexual selection, the two different plumages are haphazardly distributed with no apparent regard for male or female, age or range.

We made good progress, twisting and turning and rising up the narrowing river for mile upon mile. At one point, where the river split into two around an island, the trees on either bank were so close together that their branches touched and, over our heads, a troop of Pig-tailed macaques, on all fours, their tails slightly curled and held up in the air behind them, like those of so many cats pleased to be home, were making an aerial crossing. They scrutinised us for a moment or two, and then scampered for cover.

Further up, in a massively-buttressed oak-like tree, sat something large and furry, a rich, mahogany red back and side of fur with its head obscured by leaves. Just for a moment, I thought it might be an orang-utan, but had to admit that it was scarcely probable; we were far more likely to have caught a glimpse of a Maroon leaf monkey, Hose's Maroon langur.

In any case, it was just then that James promised to see something marvellous, having, I believe, seen it already. High up, circling in a sky which at that time of day can look almost English, heat-wave, August-blue with a fluff of clouds, were two enormous eagles, pitch-black, their tails surprisingly long: Black eagles.

The river became shallower as the day wore on and once again I had to push the boat, almost continuously. It was shattering work, heaving against the current, falling over the stones on the river-bed. The Iban were as fit as men could be, but an extra source of energy fuelled them, too; could it simply be the rice they ate, at each meal, some twelve times more than us, some twelve times more than one would have thought possible? I resolved to mimic Leon's diet in every particular.

At lunch-time, Leon harpooned a river tortoise, about eighteen inches long with a muddy black carapace and its plastron flat and blotched with yellow and black. He was stowed, sadly, beneath the duckboards of the dugout. Inghai caught yet more sebarau, and we roasted them over an open fire. Expecting to keel over like a blown bull at any moment, to explode disgustingly amongst the rocks, I forced myself to eat as much sticky, finger-gluing rice as Leon did, to the great approval of the Iban and the horror of the Fenton. Life began to seem even better, and much rounder.

Putting up the bashas that evening, I heard a rushing noise above the trees, like the wings of swans.

"Hornbills! Hornbills!"

"Tajai! Tajai!" shouted Dana, running for his gun.

"No, no, Leon. Tell him not to shoot!"

The two great birds, larger than swans, four feet across the wings, flew heavily over the river, unperturbed by our shouting. Their long tail plumes trailing, their wings making a whooshing noise with each stroke, they alternately flapped and sailed, labouring and gliding into the topmost branches of a dead tree on the far bank. Bespattered with white droppings, it was obviously a favourite perch. I watched them through the binoculars, through the small clear patch of lens which had not yet succumbed to the all-enroaching fungus growing within the tubes.

Their necks were feathery orange; the solid ivory casques, the square block-mountings on top of their bills, were red and yellow. Ruffling their feathers, they looked at us, and flapped away from view into the canopy of tree tops. But, in a moment or two, they began their extraordinary calling, a series of strong hoots getting louder and quicker and more excited and ending in a burst of dirty hilarity, *cack-cack-cack-cackle*. Other birds joined in. And then we heard a different sound, a loud succession of barking, roaring calls.

"Kenyalang!" said Dana, beaming. "Badas!"

"It's good lucks," said Leon, "it's our gawai bird. Very important bird for we Iban."

Dana called, a deep raven call, and the bird answered.

"We have very good lucks, and now we cook the turtle," said Leon.

The hornbills kept calling, allowing me to check their notes against their score in Smythies. Kenyalang was the Rhinoceros hornbill, a bird central to Iban ritual, and Tajai was indeed the Helmeted hornbill, whose ivory was once more valuable than jade, and was traded from Borneo to China certainly at the time of the first Ming Emperor, and probably long before. As for the Rhinoceros hornbill ceremonies, I resolved to screw the anthropological secrets, if there were any, out of Leon, later.

Hunks of turtle meat were a great improvement on weak sebarau flesh and strong sebarau needle-bones, but the tightly-compacted, powerful muscles were tough to eat. It was a Wrigley's Mudmint Chewing Gum Turtle. Still masticating my strip of *Trionyx subplanus* two hours later, I went to bed to read about hornbills. Hose, I decided, in *The Field-Book of a Jungle-Wallah*, had the best description of their nesting habits.

All the species build their home, for protection, in a hollow tree, communication with the outer world being by means of a slit or hole. If this opening is not at the right elevation above the floor of the nest the birds fill up the interior with leaves and twigs until it is the right height for the mother-bird to be able to sit comfortably on her eggs with her beak protruding so as to receive food. This having been arranged satisfactorily, the hen bird spreads a thin layer of feathers plucked from her own body on the built-up floor, and is then completely walled up by the male, who plasters over the opening with a sort of gummy substance which he secretes in his stomach; this substance hardens on exposure to the air and shuts in the female until her beak alone shows. In this uncomfortable position she remains a prisoner until her nestlings are from two to three weeks old, the male feeding her meanwhile with insects, fruits, seeds, and parts of frogs and lizards, all rolled up into a sort of pellet, which he throws into the expectant beak of his mate.

When feeding the female, the cock bird clings to the bark of the tree, or else perches on a convenient branch, and jerks the food into his wife's beak. I knew one instance where, the husband-bird having been shot by hunters, other males came and supported the widow. While the feeding and imprisonment process is going on, several seeds naturally are not caught by the hen, and falling to the ground germinate; by observing the growth of these, the natives can infer the age of the young birds without seeing them.

The native method of catching the mother-bird during the period of incubation is rather brutal. The tree is scaled and the entrance broken open; the frightened bird flutters up the hollow trunk but is brought down with a thorny stick which is thrust in after her and twisted about until a firm grip is obtained of both her flesh and plumage.

Hornbills make amusing and interesting pets, for they become quite tame and will follow their owner about like a dog. One that I had at Claudetown became quite an expert at catching bananas thrown him. On one occasion the late Rajah was staying with me and was surprised over his morning tea and fruit by my pet, who coolly perched on the railing of the verandah. Taken aback by the grotesque creature, he looked round for something to throw at it, but while his head was turned for a second, a whirring noise was heard and his breakfast was gone.

I fell asleep, and nightmares returned. I lay stuck fast, fat with Inghai's greasy rice, white with SAS anti-fungus skin powder, at the dark base of a hornbill-hole in some Freudian tree. There was a cracking noise above my head and the entrance burst apart. With great difficulty, the wreaths of flesh round my neck squashing against the bark, I looked up. Chotty was enlarging the opening with a meat hammer. She looked in, a thorny stick in her other hand. "Of course, it doesn't matter now he's drowned," she said, "but you should have placed yourself *behind* him on the rope."

EIGHT

The next day the river became more difficult still: an unending series of rapids and snags and boulders. The dugout seemed to increase its weight with every mile; the 120° heat, bearing down and beating off the surface of the water seemed less easy to struggle through, even when the warm water was up to one's neck. Two towels bound round my head failed to keep the sweat out of my eyes and off my glasses.

There were fewer laughs at lunch-time on the shingle. The river was too low, said Dana, the going too tough. We now needed two small canoes instead of one big one. Only Leon, immensely strong, cheerful and affectionate, was undaunted. He was obviously a champion river-hunter, too: while we lay, exhausted, in the shade of a jungle chestnut tree, he disappeared, swimming underwater up an adjacent creek. Half an hour later he returned, towing a fresh trophy. It was much longer than he was: a big Water monitor, a black and yellow prehistoric dragon with a long forked tongue which it protruded like a snake. Dana and Leon pulled it up the bank. It stood four-square, clear of the ground, hissing, and lashing its long tail, the harpoon stuck through its side. Dana drew his parang and killed it with a blow to the head.

The lizard strapped into the dugout, we set off again. It was too arduous to notice much—for hour upon hour I was only really conscious of the whirling water, the side of the boat and my own gripping positions on the gunwale. But then the country began to open out, the big trees stepped back from the bank; rolling hills, covered with nothing but young scrub-jungle, stretched away to a forest horizon. The Iban looked about them uneasily. There was no mark of all this on our secret government maps.

We continued on our way for a mile or so and then, glancing up, I found myself looking into the big brown eyes of a girl on the bank beside us. She was standing in a loose clump of bamboo, her fine black hair falling over her bare shoulders and breasts.

"Kayan?" shouted Dana.

The girl turned and fled.

A little further on, four men, in two small canoes, were setting nets.

"Kayan?" Dana repeated.

"Kenyah!" shouted the men, much insulted. They yelled instructions above the noise of the water, pointing upriver.

"Can you understand them, Leon?"

"No," said Leon, uncharacteristically quiet. "These are not our peoples."

The river meandered, grew broader and more shallow, and then entered a very long straight reach. A paradise was disclosed. An inland kingdom, secluded almost beyond reach, of padi fields and banana trees, palms and coconuts, lay in its own wide valley, surrounded by jungle hills; a huge longhouse, its atap roof blending into the landscape, was set back from the left bank of the river, about three miles off; some forest giants had been left standing, here and there, and on one of these a pair of Brahminy kites were sitting, the birds of Singalang Burong, King of the Gods.

Cheered by amused men in light fishing canoes and by families from their farms on the banks, it took us two hours to manhandle the heavy dugout up to the beach beneath the longhouse.

About to wade ashore, Dana stopped me emphatically, pointing me to my place on the duckboards.

"We must waits," said Leon. "This not our country."

About sixty children watched us silently from the bank. Some of their mothers, their ear-lobes, weighted by brass rings, dangling down below their shoulders, watched too. In about a quarter of an hour, after much to-ing and fro-ing, the chief's son arrived and formally invited us to set foot on his tribal lands.

Heaving the Bergens on to our backs we followed him towards the longhouse along a network of paths laid out between the padi stores, huts on stilts, each with its own ladder and with a close-fitting down-turned plate of wood set around each stilt to keep out the rats. The settlement was obviously large and well-organised. Even the dogs looked young and healthy. And the longhouse, when we reached it, was spectacular. Massively constructed on tree-trunk piles and a forest of lesser stilts, it was about three hundred yards long, the main floor set fifteen feet from the ground. Dark, hairy, boar-like pigs, indistinguishable from the Wild bearded pigs of the jungle, rooted and grunted amongst the garbage between the poles; chickens, the cockerels looking as magnificent as the ancestral Jungle fowl, scratched about amongst the pigs, and favourite dogs, stretched out on the side of the verandah, lolled their heads over the edge of the bamboo platform and observed our arrival with mild interest.

Climbing a slippery notched log up to a longhouse with a sixty-pound Bergen on one's back is not easy, and I went up the muddy trunk almost on all fours, holding on hard with both hands. The Iban and the chief's son paused while James and I took our shoes off; we then crossed the outer apron and the roofed verandah and were ushered into the chief's quarters. The room stretched, at right angles, back from the line of the longhouse for about a hundred feet. It was cross-beamed and triangularly roofed like a barn, the huge timbers cross-cut into one another and lashed with rattan. There were several sleeping platforms, some with curtains, some with bamboo partitions round them, down one side of the room. The chief's son, smaller, fairer-skinned than the Iban, but just as muscular and just as digni-fied, indicated a patch of floor where we might sleep. Dana and he, to their mutual delight, began to talk, albeit with no great fluency.

"They very clever mens," said Leon, "they both talk Kayan."

"Can you talk Kayan?"

Leon grinned.

"Only very dirty words. A girl she told them to me. A very silly Kayan girls. But I talk English."

"Well, you'll have to translate *everything*. You'll have to help us—you ask Dana what they're saying."

Leon and Dana talked rapidly in Iban.

"The son of the chief says he very sorries. Almost all the people are in the fields, but they come back tonight. The chief is away on the Mahakam."

"The Mahakam?"

"These people they come from there. They come fifteen years ago. This good land, very good."

So they had crossed over the mountains from the great Mahakam basin, from Indonesia, from the river that flowed south-east, into the Makassar Strait.

"We have fun tonight," said Leon.

I awoke instantly from a passing reverie, a realisation that we must be within striking distance of the centre of Borneo, perhaps almost within reach of the wild, nomadic, primitive peoples, the Ukit, the men who could tell us, if anyone could, whether or no the Borneo rhinoceros was still to be found.

"Hey Leon," I said, a little too anxiously, "step outside a minute, will you? I've something very important to tell you."

"Eh?"

"Come on."

Out on the verandah, I grabbed his tattooed arm. "Look—don't tell James, because he wouldn't like it, he's so modest. But, in England, he's *very* famous. He is the poet of all the tribe, the chief poet in all England. His *whole life* is making songs. That's what he does all day. You understand? He *sings songs*. And he dances. He knows *all* the dances."

Leon was genuinely excited, immensely impressed.

"So look Leon, between now and tonight, tell everyone—or else James will just sit there—you tell everyone, via Dana, that James is the greatest poet in all England and that when it's our turn to dance and sing, they must shout for James. Okay? Will you do that?"

"He very great man," said Leon, "very old. Very serious man. I tell Dana."

We began to unpack; and a crowd started to gather. The oldest woman I had yet seen in Borneo, squatting on the floor, her wrinkled breasts, and her ear-lobes, hanging forlornly, her attitude one of exaggerated distress, was alternately touching my leg and theatrically placing her hands over her eyes. I assumed that, sensibly enough, she found the sight of me painful beyond endurance and wanted this white tramp out of her drawing-room, fast. After all, with a half-grown beard, river-and-sweat-soaked shirt, water-frayed trousers and socks, and already inescapably possessed of the sweet, fetid, rotting smell of the jungle, I was even less of a truffle for the senses than usual. But I suddenly realised that she was asking for help. Her old eyes were bloodshot, her eyelids swollen. Feeling useful and needed, I pulled out my medicine pack and found the antibiotic eye drops. Smiling broadly she disclosed her gums. Not a tooth to be seen. I squeezed in some drops and she clapped her hands.

A mother pressed forward, holding up her baby's arm. There was an angry red mound of infection on it, just below the shoulder-joint. Perhaps this was the ringworm that Harrisson wrote about.

"Kurap?" I asked.

She nodded, impatiently. I put Savlon and a dressing on the wound, covering up the skin which was split like a rotten tomato, and weeping like one. A queue of mothers and children formed; we dressed hundreds of cuts that had gone septic, small ulcers, patches of skin fungus, rashes. And then the men began to trickle in. They mimed, with a suppleness, a balletic grace that would have impressed Nijinsky, excruciating, disabling back pain; with eyes as big and bright as those of a fox hunting in the dusk they indicated that they were suffering from the kind of headaches that amount to concussion; with contortions that would have torn Houdini into spare ribs they demonstrated that their stomachs had ceased to function, that they were debilitated almost beyond assistance.

"Multivite," I announced, with great solemnity.

"Alka-seltzer," said James, as one who practised it.

I put two bright orange pills in each extended palm. Some swallowed. Some chewed. Everyone looked happy.

The eight tablets, as white and round and efficacious as sacred slices of pig tusk, sat in the bottom of James's mess-tin. Gurgle, gurgle went his upturned water bottle, and the roundels spun and bubbled and talked to each other and grew as thin as excised circles of feather cut from the very tip of the tail of the hornbill. Throwing up spray, foaming like the river in a rapid, the water rose up in the tin. The Kenyah crowded round tight, and looked in.

"Drink," said James, handing it to the first man and staring at him like a shaman. The patient shut his eyes, mumbled something, and took a mouthful. "Aaah!" he gasped, passing it on, wiping the fizz from his lips. "Aah!" said everyone in turn, straightening out at once, squaring their powerful shoulders. There would be no backache tonight.

Trying to resume our unpacking and, most pressing of all, to change into our dry clothes, I dislodged the sealed bag of picture-postcards of the Queen on horseback, Trooping the Colour. An idea presented itself: the Sovereign would save me from undue scrutiny in the transition between pairs of trousers.

"Look," I said, "this is for you. Here is our Tuai Rumah, our chief in England."

"Inglang!" said the children. The cards were sheeny and metallic, the kind that change the position of their subjects as their own position is changed against the light.

I gave one to a little boy. He looked at it with amazed delight: he turned it this way and that; he scratched it and waited to see what would happen; he whipped it over, to catch a glimpse of Her Majesty from the back. Small hands thrust up like a clump of bamboo; the old woman, annoyed, demanded a pile for herself. If the children had one each, the men wanted more than one each. In five minutes, four hundred mementoes of the Empire disappeared.

There were now so many people in the room that I really wanted a photograph: with, I imagined, great stealth, I held a Fuji to my stomach, pointed it in the right direction, looked the other way myself, and pressed the button. Chaos ensued. Children howled, the women pulled their sarongs over their breasts, the men looked annoyed.

"Quick, quick—get the Polaroid," hissed James.

With an elaborate enactment of deep apology, followed by circus gestures promising fun to come, great tricks, something quite different, and not at all offensive, I drew out the Polaroid and loaded it. The grey box would take away their image, I tried to suggest with both hands, and then give it back again. They looked dubious. I had behaved badly once, and was not really to be trusted.

The Polaroid flashed; we waited; the box whirred; the tray slid forward and proffered its wet card. I laid it on the floor, waving their fingers away. Slowly, it grew colours, like bacteria in a dish of culture. The room was very silent. They watched the outlines of heads and shoulders appear; features became defined. Suddenly they pointed to the card and to each other. Wild hilarity erupted. They clapped and clapped. They ran off to change into their best clothes and we, at last, put on our dry trousers. Only the old woman was left to grimace in astonishment, or disgust, at the whiteness, or the hairiness, of our legs.

Proudly wearing garish sarongs or Chinese shorts and tee-shirts which had been traded downriver in the rainy season, presumably, for turtles or deer or pig, for camphor or gutta-percha or rattan or pepper, they arranged themselves into family groups, forcing me to shuttle their images in and their pictures out, until the Polaroid grew hot and all the film was finished.

"What a lot of children everyone has," I observed to Leon.

"No, no," said Leon, "the mothers and the fathers—they die. My own parents, they die too, sickness, or cutting trees, shick-shick," said Leon, miming the curving descent of a parang blade, "or in the river, bang heads on the rocks, or poison-fish, or in the jungle, hunting. You have cut. You have boil. Very painful. You have very good lucks to get better. Then you must be adopted. I adopted. My uncle and my aunt. Very kind peoples. Or the peoples in the bileks [rooms] next door. They must take the children."

So these magnificent warrior-farmers, I thought, looking round at so much health and so much glowing muscle, at so many beautiful faces and breasts and smiles and jangling ear-rings, are the product of evolution by natural selection almost in its crudest sense.

The chief's son ushered everyone out of the huge room. We must be hungry, he said (we were); his mother and his sisters had cooked the monitor lizard (perhaps we were not quite that hungry). At the far end of the room there was a fire of split logs with a massive piece of ironwood for a hearth. A series of pots were suspended above it, and the smoke made its way out through a propped-open flap in the roof.

The girls left our mess-tins and plates in a circle round a piled bowl of rice and the hindquarters of the monitor lizard, and then withdrew. Dana served me a helping of tail, the last ten inches of it, or thereabouts; and the resin lamps flickered, and the sows and boars and piglets grunted and squealed on the rubbish and pig-shit below the floorboards; and the geckoes chick-chacked to each other in the roof spaces like mating sparrows; and I realised that the yellow-and-black-skinned monitor lizard tail would not disappear from my tin, as custom demanded, until I ate it myself.

"Makai! Makai!" said Dana.

The flesh was yellow and softish and smelt bad, very like the stray chunks of solid matter in the effluvia one sees in England on an unwashed pavement outside a public house late on a Saturday night. I eased it off the small vertebrae, mixed it into the sticky rice, and told myself that even this particular meal would all be over one day.

The Iban ate fast and went out for a swim in the river and a wash. We finished our supper, more or less, but felt momentarily far too sick to swim in the dark. The girls cleared everything away. Returning, looking very clean, Dana, Leon and Inghai put on their most dazzling trousers and tee-shirts. They then, with great deliberation, took turns with Dana's piece of broken mirror and his rusty tweezers to pluck out any hairs that might have sprouted unbeknown upon their chins or cheeks. Leon sported a straggly thin moustache which he later shaved away, but in general the races of Borneo are almost hairless, and they dislike any growth on the face intensely. They

64

certainly disliked ours. It amused me to think that Darwin himself had run into logical trouble attempting to argue away this awkward anomaly in his scheme for the differential advancement of races. "Some races are much more hairy than others," he writes in *The Descent of Man*, "especially the males; but it must not be assumed that the more hairy races, such as the European, have retained their primordial condition more completely than the naked races, such as the Kalmucks or Americans. It is more probable that the hairiness of the former is due to partial reversion; for characters which have been at some former period long inherited, are always apt to return. We have seen that idiots are often very hairy, and they are able to revert in other characters to a lower animal type."

Suddenly, a wave of sound made its way into the room from the long gallery outside, simple melodies beautifully sung, a clear chorus of young voices which swept over us and out through the thin bamboo walls to the padi fields and the jungle beyond. Surprised, we went to investigate. The youth of the longhouse was assembled in rows, singing hymns in Kenyah.

"Roman Catholics," said Leon. "Very good. But we have fun later."

"Who converted them?"

"The missionaries of course. The other side. They bring it with them."

It was an odd idea indeed, Roman Catholic missionaries in ex-Dutch Borneo, at the very headwaters of the Mahakam. A middle-aged man beat time with a stick, a battered green hymn book in his other hand. The singing went on and on; but eventually the meeting was over, and the flaming youth of Nanga Sinyut dispersed.

We were very tired. It was all too confusing; the river seemed to have spun cat's-cradles of pain out of all the muscle fibres in my calves and back; and the monitor-lizard's tail was still gently whisking, from side to side, in my stomach. I took a long pull at the arak-can and lay down on the floor of the chief's room. The huge cross-beams of the roof bucked and twisted and stuck fast on some celestial river floating over my head: I fell asleep.

"Come on," shouted James, from a bank far away to my right, "get up! There's going to be a welcome party."

Staggering out, wanting to sleep as never before, I looked around, and wished I was somewhere else. The gallery was packed. The lamps had been lit. Tuak was being drunk. A long, uninviting space had been cleared in front of part of the line of longhouse doors; and around its three sides sat an expectant audience.

Leon and Inghai, looking fresh and eager, beckoned us to the back row. Dana was nowhere to be seen. He was, as Leon explained, as befitted his high and kingly status, drinking with the deputy chief of all the Kenyah on the Baleh, and was not to be disturbed, because, being Absolute Chief of all the Iban of Kapit District, he had many cares, and would soon be taking a sleeps.

We were given a glass of tuak. A tray of huge cone-shaped cheroots of Kenyah tobacco wrapped in leaves and each tied with a bow of leaf-strips was passed round; a sinuous young girl put ours in our mouths and lit them with a taper. I noticed that Leon was wearing his large and flashy, supposedly waterproof, digital watch. After its first celebratory dive with Leon into the depths of the Rajang this watch had ceased to tell the time, but it would still, if shaken violently enough, and to Leon's unvarying delight, sound its alarm.

The musicians sat in front of us. An old man held a keluri, a dried gourd shaped like a chemical retort but held upwards, and with six bamboo pipes projecting in a bundle from its bulb; a group of young men sat ready with a bamboo harp (a tube of bamboo with raised strips cut from its surface), a bamboo xylophone, a bamboo flute, and a single stringed instrument, a dugout-canoe-like sounding box carved from a single block of wood, the string so heavy it had to be pulled with an iron hook.

The chief's son entered, transformed. On his head he wore a war-helmet, a woven rattan cap set with black and yellow and crimson beads, topped with six long black and white plumes from the tail of the Helmeted hornbill. He was dressed in a war-coat, made from the skin of the largest cat in Borneo, the Clouded leopard. His head placed through an opening at the front of the skin, the bulk stretched down his back, and on to it were fastened row upon row of Rhinoceros hornbill feathers. Around his waist, slung on a silver belt and sheathed in a silver scabbard, was a parang to outshine all other parangs, its hilt intricately carved in horn from the antler of the kijang, the big Borneo deer. In his left hand, his arm crooked behind it, he carried a long shield, pointed at both ends, and from the centre of which a huge mask regarded us implacably, its eyes red, its teeth the painted tusks of the wild boar. Thick black tufts of hair hung in neat lines down either edge and across the top and bottom, tufts of hair which, we were led to believe, had long ago been taken from the scalps of heads cut off in battle. Laying the ancient, and presumably fragile, shield carefully against the wall, the warrior took up his position at the centre of the floor. He crouched down and, at a nod from the man on the base string, a hollow, complicated, urgent, rhythmic music began. With exaggerated movements, his thigh muscles bunching and loosening, his tendons taut, a fierce concentration on his face, the chief's son turned slowly in time with the music, first on one foot and then on another, rising, inch by inch, to his own height, apparently peering over some imaginary cover. Sighting the enemy, he crouched again, and then, as the music quickened, he drew his bright parang and leapt violently forward, weaving and dodging, with immense exertion, cutting and striking, parrying unseen blows with his mimed shield. For a small second, his ghostly foe was off-guard, tripped on the shingle, and the heir to the Lordship of all the Kenyah of Nanga Sinyut claimed his victory with one malicious blow.

Everyone clapped and cheered, and so did I. Five young girls rushed forward to take off the hero's hornbill helmet, and war-coat, and parang. It was wonderful. The girls were very beautiful. All was right with the world. And then I realised, as a Rajah Brooke's birdwing took a flap around my duodenum, that the beautiful girls, in a troop, were coming, watched by all the longhouse, for me.

"You'll be all right," said James, full of tuak. "Just do your thing. Whatever it is."

Strapped into the war-coat and the parang, the hornbill feathers on my head, I had a good idea. It would be a simple procedure to copy the basic steps that the chief's son had just shown us. There really was not much to it, after all. The music struck up, sounding just a little bit stranger than it had before.

I began the slow crouch on one leg, turning slightly. Perhaps, actually, this was a mistake, I decided. Ghastly pains ran up my thighs. Terminal cramp hit both buttocks at once. Some silly girl began to titter. A paraplegic wobble spread down my back. The silly girl began to laugh. Very slowly, the floor came up to say hello, and I lay down on it. There was uproar in the longhouse. How very funny, indeed.

Standing up, I reasoned that phase two would be easier. Peering over the imaginary boulder, I found myself looking straight into the eyes of an old man on the far side of the verandah. The old fool was crying with laughter, his ridiculous long ears waggling about. Drawing the parang, which was so badly aligned that it stuck in the belt and nearly took my fingers off, I advanced upon the foe, jumping this way and that, feeling dangerous. The old man fell off his seat. There was so much misplaced mirth, so much plain howling, that I could not hear the music, and so perhaps my rhythm was not quite right.

"Redsi!" came an unmistakable shout, "why don't you improvise?"

Stabbed in the back just as I was about to take my very first head, I spun round violently to glare at the Fenton. I never actually saw him, because the cord of the war-helmet, not used to such movements, slipped up over the back of my head, and the helmet itself, flying forward, jammed fast over my face. Involuntarily, I took a deep gasp of its sweat-smooth rattan interior, of the hair of generations of Kenyah warriors who had each been desperate to impress the girls of their choice. It was an old and acrid smell.

The boards were shaking. The audience was out of control. And then, just in time, before suffocation set in, the five girls, grossly amused, set me free.

"Go and get James," I spluttered, "you go and get James."

"Now you sing song," shouted Leon.

"No, no—James sing songs."

"Jams!" shouted Leon, remembering his mission.

"Jams!" The longhouse reverberated. "Jams! Jams!" Leon had done his work well.

With great theatrical presence, offering almost no resistance to the five young girls, James processed on to the stage. The Kenyah fell silent. T.D. Freeman, in his work on Iban augury, tells us that the King of the Gods, Singalang Burong, may well be encountered in dreams. There is no mistaking him. He is almost as old as the trees, awe-inspiring, massive of body, and, a characteristic which puts his identity beyond doubt, completely bald. Judging by the slightly uneasy, deferential, expectant faces around me, Bali Penyalong, the High God of the Kenyah, was but a different name for the same deity.

The attendants withdrew. James, resplendent in leopard skin and hornbill feathers, looked even more solemn than is his habit. With the accumulated experience of many thousands of evenings at the theatre, of years of drama criticism, he regarded his audience; his huge brown eyes appeared to fix on everyone in turn. There was some backward shuffling in the front row. A dog whimpered.

68

The music began, a little shakily. James, in time with the music, began to mime. He was hunting something, in a perfunctory way; he made rootling movements with his head, and grunted. He was hunting a pig. Evidently successful, he butchered his quarry, selected the joint he had in mind, hung the carcase from a hook in the roof and betook himself to his ideal kitchen. Passion entered the show; James began to concentrate; his gestures quickened and the mesmerised musicians increased their tempo. He scored the pork; he basted it; he tied it with string; he made extraordinarily complex sauces; he cooked potatoes and sprouts and peas and beans and broccoli and *zucchini*, I think, until they were *fritti*. After many a tasting and many an alchemical manoeuvre with a *batterie de cuisine* decidedly better than Magny's, James deemed the gravy to be perfect. The apple sauce was plentiful. The decanted Burgundy was poured into a glass. James looked fondly at his creation and began to eat. The crackling crackled between his teeth. The warriors of the Kenyah, as if they had been present at a feast of the Gods, rose to their feet and burped. Everybody cheered.

"Jams very hungry," said Leon to me confidentially, "he must eat more rices."

James held up a hand. Everyone sat down again, cross-legged.

"And now," he announced, "we will have a sing-song."

"Inglang song! Inglang song!" shouted Inghai, wildly excited, and full of arak.

And then James really did astonish me. To the beat of the big string he launched into a rhyming ballad, a long spontaneous poem about our coming from a far country, entering the Rajang from the sea, about the pleasures of the Baleh and the danger of the rapids and the hospitality of the strongest, the most beautiful people in all the world, the Kenyah of Nanga Sinyut.

I clapped as wildly as Inghai. "Bravo Jams!" I shouted; "Bravo Jams!" mimicked Inghai; "Bravo! Bravo!" sang the Kenyah.

James indicated that he was tired; he pillowed his black-and-white-plumed head on his hands. But it was no use. We wanted more songs. We wanted so many, in fact, that I discovered, to my amazement, that he knew almost every popular and music-hall song back to about 1910 and that he could adapt their tunes to the vagaries of the bamboo gourd-pipes with professional ease.

James was saved, just before he collapsed from exhaustion, when the longhouse clown stood up, jealous of his great success. The helmet and coat were laid aside, and James sat down. But my annoyance was short-lived. People began to laugh before the clown had done anything at all, and it soon became obvious that he was a very witty Fool indeed.

With exaggerated seriousness, he sat on the floor, his legs out-stretched; he put on an imaginary hat and he fastened his imaginary shirt-cuffs. He looked about, unconcerned, like a great chief.

"It's Jams!" said Leon, "It's Jams in the boat! He very serious man!"

"Jams!" said the Kenyah, laughing with recognition and approval.

The clown then got out of the longboat and became a Neander-thaler, struggling in the river, pulling the dugout this way and that, always getting it wrong, unable to walk and push at the same time, his movements constantly directed, with a frantic exasperation of con-tradictory gestures, by Dana and Leon and Inghai. There were roars of laughter.

"It's Redmon!" said Leon. "He very fats!"

The chief's son then stood up and announced something. The long gallery became quiet again. He pointed to about fifteen men, in turn, who followed him on to the floor. They were all young and eager, bodily alert, absurdly fit. Long-backed, with fairly short, lavishly muscled limbs, they looked like athletes at the peak of their careers, assembling at the Olympics for the men's pentathlon.

"They all bachelors," whispered Leon. "They not yet picked their womens."

The men formed into a single line, by order of height. And a completely different kind of music began, violent, aggressive, with a menacing and insistent beat. They walked slowly forward, unsmiling, stamping their feet, looking rhythmically to either side, intent. This, I realised, was the dance described in Hose, albeit the protagonists were wearing shorts and singlets:

The bigger boys are taught to take part in the dance in which the return from the warpath is dramatically represented. This is a musical march rather than a dance. A party of young men in full war-dress form up in single line; the leader, and perhaps two or three others, play the battle march on the *keluri*. The line advances slowly up the gallery, each man turning half about at every third step, the even numbers turning to the one hand, the odd to the other hand, alternately, and all stamping together as they complete the turn at each third step. The turning to right and left symbolises the alert guarding of the heads which are supposed to be carried by the victorious warriors.

After five march-pasts, as I was deciding that this would not be a sensible longhouse to attack even if one really was in the SAS, everyone relaxed, and we were invited to join the line. James picked up the rhythm at once, but I found even these steps difficult, falling over my boots. All the girls giggled.

"Redmon," said Leon, when we sat down again, "you so big, your feet too far from your head."

"That's it. That's exactly what it is."

There was a pause.

"Or, maybe," said Leon, "you so fats you can't see them."

Leon, with gross bad manners, uncrossed his legs, lay flat out on the floor, and laughed at his own joke, re-directing his attention, sharply, only when the unmarried girls stood up.

Gracefully, shyly, the young girls aligned themselves.

"Look at that one," said Leon, "look at that one in the pink sarong. Redmon. Just *look* at that one."

"Behave yourself," I said, testily. "This is no time for one of your jumps. You'll get us all killed."

"She the moon in the sky," said Leon.

The girls, to a delicate, lilting dance-tune, began their own movement across the long stage and back again; lithe, slender, very young, they were indeed lovely to look at; and their dance was deliciously fragile after the violence of the men. With small, flowing movements of their wrists and fingers, all in synchrony, their arms rippling, their supple bodies undulating slightly, they mimicked the leisurely flight of the hornbill. The forward step on the beat outlined the legs beneath their folded-down sarongs. The gentle, backward swaying, on the pause, revealed the tight breasts beneath their tee-shirts.

Leon's eyes were wide, as wide as they had been when he shot his turtle. I blew in his ear.

"Shush," said Leon. "You be quiets. Now we watch."

Looking round to poke Inghai, I saw that he was asleep, curled up on the floor, still holding his arak mug in both hands. All the men were very quiet.

Far too soon, the dance was over. We clapped, adoringly, sentimentally, soppily, feeling a little weak. The girls, blushing, scurried to their seats and giggled. But the girl in the pink sarong returned, carrying two huge bunches of hornbill feathers. They were strapped to her wrists, set out and fixed like an open fan. Her features were strikingly beautiful, certainly; her hair, about a foot longer than that of the other girls, was combed down, loose and fine, black and silky, to her waist. Her looped ear-lobes, weighted with rings, hung down only to the base of her smooth neck, soft and brown in the light of the lamp. The tattoos on her arms were only half-complete and, as tattooing begins in a girl's tenth year and continues in small bouts at regular intervals (otherwise the pain of the operation would be insupportable and the ensuing inflammation probably fatal) she could be, I calculated, no more than fourteen or fifteen years old.

"Leon," I said, "she's far too young. She's only fourteen."

"What is it?" said Leon. "What is it? You sit stills. You be quiets. Now we watch."

However young, she danced with tremulous invitation, a slow, yearning, graceful dance, the long fan feathers sweeping over her body in alternating curves, a dance that began from a crouching position and opened gradually upwards as she rose, inch by inch, a celestial bird, some as-yet-undiscovered hornbill of paradise, flying upwards towards the sun, towards the bright world where Bali Penyalong is Lord of the House.

"This is really something," whispered James, holding his head in both hands, gazing at her. And then, perhaps remembering his professional self, his column inches, "she *really*, *really* knows what she's doing."

The two fans of the tail feathers of the Rhinoceros hornbill, at the end of her outstretched arms, joined above her head. She stood at her full height, little, curved, lissome, beautiful. We clapped and clapped.

And then, suddenly looking straight at us, giving us a small charge of our own internal electricity, a conger eel uncurling in the guts, she walked into the audience with every eye upon her and pulled Leon to his feet.

Leon's brown face grew browner and browner. He was blushing. He was suffusing, uncontrollably, with blood, and surprise, with fright and pride, with increasing vigour and overpowering lust.

She tied him, very slowly, into the helmet and the war-coat, lingering over every knot, staring steadily into his eyes, hanging the belt around his waist with both her hands, arranging the silver parang so that it hung neatly down the outside of his right thigh.

Leon, taller and darker than the Kenyah, and just as fit, stood like a warrior; and this was his reward, I realised. For Leon, conqueror of the river, as she must have heard, had proved his manhood and his spontaneous, natural courage as surely as if he had arrived at Nanga Sinyut with a severed head. In our eyes, and probably in theirs, he had done much better: he had saved one, and a particularly fine specimen, too, a Bald godhead rescued from a blow amongst the rocks.

Still fired with inspiration, his face growing even darker, he nodded to his little muse in lordly fashion as she returned to her seat. He then, I am sure, executed the finest dance of his life. To the frantic music of open combat, he somersaulted backwards; he cartwheeled from side to side; he cut heads like corn; he lunged and feinted and dodged behind his imaginary shield; he twisted and spun through the air faster than flying spears. For his new love, he topped whole armies. He moved with such energy that black and white banded wheels, images of hornbill feathers, arcs and lines, seemed to hang in the murk all around him, fading and appearing in the flicker of the lamp.

Finally, the music stopped and Leon, shiny with sweat and grasping, I assume, a bundle of heads, strode with them to the side of his beloved and dropped them in her lap. In the stunned, short pause before the clapping began I heard an odd noise. It was not a gecko. It was Leon's watch. It was as shaken and over-excited as he was. *Beeeep-beeeep-beeeep* it said.

Leon, disrobed, momentarily speechless with exertion and wanting a rest, woke up Inghai with his foot. Ingy-Pingy, bleary but good-natured, not at all sure where he was, did the kind of kung-fu which a dormouse might do, on arising from hibernation. He yawned and uncurled and stretched his arms and legs full out a bit, and then went back to sleep.

The formal gathering broke up into small groups, drinking and laughing and telling stories. The largest circle grew around James. The Kenyah sat at his feet in rings, listening to his bizarre tales of life in England. They studied his expressive face and his agitated gestures, laughing at the right moments, tingling, when required, at the voice from the Hammer House of Horror, just as if they knew where Rugley was, or were connoisseurs of murder, or understood two words of what he said.

Maybe the arak and tuak were beginning to tell on me. My legs seemed to have contracted elephantiasis. It was difficult to focus. The longhouse pitched a bit, like an anchored canoe. Or maybe I was simply coming to the end of the longest day I ever hope to traverse.

As if from a long way off, I heard James issue a solemn warning to his audience:

> The Butcher bird, or Red-backed shrike
> Should not be trusted with your bike
> The pump and light he whips away
> And takes the spokes to spike his prey.

It was an entirely new, unpublished Fenton poem, I realised, dimly. But whatever it was, it was beyond me. And so were the Kenyah. I staggered, luckily, the right way off the verandah, through the correct bilek door, and found my patch of board. Through the wooden wall I could hear James singing songs, parcelling out the verses, teaching the Kenyah English. I fell asleep.

• NINE •

I awoke very suddenly, well before dawn. There were no cocks crowing; the pigs were snoring under the floor; the dogs were silent. Even the geckoes were asleep. But there was a light coming towards me, a taper-light. Someone was approaching from the very back of the room by the kitchen. It was a small, rustly, floaty, pinkish, graceful sort of figure. Leon lay a foot to my right, asleep. She knelt silently down and tugged his foot. Leon stirred.

"Shussh," said the young girl, pulling him to his feet.

Leon muttered something in Iban.

"Shussh," she said, and led him behind a partition on my left.

There were subdued giggles, murmurings, rustlings, kisses, squeaks. And then, it seemed, three hundred yards of longhouse began to shake. Leon, single-handed, with only a very little tender help, I thought, will have the whole lot down like a timberyard. The cross-beams rubbed back and forth on their supports. The joists strained at their rattan loops. The piles, perhaps, deep down below, thrust in and out of the earth. And Leon's watch spoke his triumph into the night: *Beeeep-beeeep-beeeep-beeeep.*

No one seemed to hear. There were happy giggles to my left. The watch became quiescent. And then the tremors of Leon's earthquake shook Nanga Sinyut to its foundations all over again. I got up and crept out for a swim.

The dawn was not fully visible. It was the time of day the Iban call Empliau bebungi, "the calling of the gibbons", well after Dini ari dalam, "dawn deep down", and just before Tampak tanah, "to see the ground". I made my way down the indistinct paths towards the river.

A "swim" in Borneo is always a euphemism for something else: a wash, or worse. Taking the upstream track I soon came to the well-worn steps, cut into the mud bank, which led down to the river.

Wading in, as the hanging mist over the river began to lighten and lift, I knew I was in the right place, the men's bathing area. I knew because it was a superior position, about fifty yards upriver from the women's area, where they swam, and where they collected the tribe's water; and I knew because the catfish swarmed round me, brushing my thighs with their long whiskers, nuzzling my y-fronts with their soft snouts, wanting me to take them down, hungry for their breakfast. A bit unnerved by their intimate attention I swam a little way off, into an upstream eddy by the bank, and there, luckily, all alone, I learned by personal experience the most important lesson of all for the tranquil conduct of life in the jungle: never, ever, shit in a whirlpool. It is a terrible decision to have to make, whether to duck or jump.

Sitting about on the river boulders to try and squeeze a little water out of my pants (bathing naked is not done in Borneo—the men go to great lengths not to expose themselves in public, and, besides, every little boy and girl is dying to know if your willy is as white as your nose and will hide in any available bush in an attempt to settle the point) I re-dressed in my dry clothes, washed my wet ones and left them on the rocks to dry, an automatic process which would begin at about 8 a.m. at Mansan jimbio, "time to dry things in the sun".

Feeling smug, lighter, and energetic, I set off to return to the longhouse, wondering secretly if James would perform in the river in front of everybody, like a man, or whether he would confer with himself and decide upon a policy of costiveness.

Musing on such deep concerns as the sky changed from orange to pale yellow to deep blue, I took the wrong path, the downstream way along the river bank rather than the men's route back to the longhouse. Hearing laughter and splashing and the shrieks of children I realised that I had unwittingly come upon the women's bathing place, by a little-used secondary path, and that I was still concealed from them by bamboo clumps, young palms and reed-like grasses. Feeling no more than a little ashamed of myself, I crept off the track and peered through the vegetation. An enormous tree had been thrown into the shallows and abandoned by some past flood, its great bulk forming a breakwater to the current and a safe lagoon in which to swim. It rose gently out of the water, and its branches were so many gnarled and tapering diving-boards for about twenty very young, very excited children, who swarmed up its trunk, ran out over the river, jumped in, swam to the bank, and then repeated the process, yelling all the while. Their mothers, slim and supple and half-naked and almost equally at home in the pool, were washing themselves and their sarongs, diving to wet their long black hair, collecting water in gourds, or in long segments of bamboo to carry home in baskets on their backs, or, a little way downstream, squatting near the river bank. Further out, a Brahminy kite, obviously a bird it was taboo to blowpipe, was quartering the river, gliding and flapping on its broad brown wings, fishing.

I returned to the proper path and walked back to the longhouse, past friendly groups of Kenyah men on the way to their stretch of water. Everyone was awake. Plumes of smoke rose in a regular row from the fireplaces at the back of the longhouse, straight up into the sky.

In the chief's room, the breakfast rice was boiling in iron cauldrons; and, just for us, a greasy stew of monitor lizard was exhaling its warm and stale breath from a Chinese cooking pot. It was a bit like the smell a dentist releases when he opens up an abscess to drain it. Feeling queasy, I was suddenly attacked by stomach cramps. Perhaps the feared moment had come at last? Perhaps the Borneo diarrhoea that gives you two minutes crawling time between the onset of heavyweight boxing in the stomach and a punch through the anal sphincter had finally searched me out? I got to my Bergen, found the right plastic bag with shaky hands, and, with a swig of cool chlorine water from the SAS bottle, swallowed two Strepto-triad and three codeine phosphate pills.

I sat very still, and, gradually, the pain began to subside.

"Makai?" asked Leon, sitting down cross-legged to rice and monitor with Dana and Inghai and a silent, hung-over James.

I shook my head.

"You the running shits," said Leon, without a moment's hesitation, thumping his stomach to show me where it hurt. "Me too, very often." And thereupon he began to eat square yards of rice, acres of haunch of lizard; Don Giovanni must have been a horrible sight at breakfast, I thought.

Leaning back against one of the ironwood uprights, I had time to look slowly at the contents of the room. These people were Iron Age farmers. They were as primitive in their methods, perhaps, as the inhabitants of Skara Brae or the builders of Stonehenge. But, amongst the spears and blowpipes, the head-dresses, the leopard-skin coat, the decorated baskets, the closely woven padi-bins, the mats and tapestries, the wooden tools and crude axes, there were some very odd trophies indeed, prized relics of trading expeditions. There were eight tins of Brasso neatly arranged in a corner. A picture of the last Pope but one was impaled on a wall with four fish-hooks. A dusty cassette-player sat on the floor with two tapes of pop music beside it; a sewing machine, gold letters on its barrel proclaiming it to be *The Standard*, sat on show on a table; and behind it, most intriguing of all, there was a globe.

The pigs snortled and squealed under the floor; dogs, being gathered for a hunting expedition, yelped; the Iban went off to inspect the boat and debate the river level; James took out his notebook and *Les Misérables*; the rhythmic, soothing noise of the women pounding padi on the verandah began; the boxers in my stomach, still hitting each other feebly, were obviously in a clinch, and tiring; and I fell asleep myself.

Some hours or minutes later, I was shaken awake. An old man clutched me by the arm. He pointed at the medicine bag and tugged at my shirt. He was obviously much distressed and I followed him out into the gallery, carrying the first aid kit. Along the great raised passageway women were pounding padi by the bilek doors. Standing in pairs with heavy poles as tall as themselves, they alternately struck the rice, held in an ironwood trough at their feet. Their backs straightened and dipped, their hair fell over their shoulders, their breasts rose and flattened on the uplift, and fell, forward and full, on the downward stroke. Leon's girl, his moon in the sky, extraordinarily beautiful, smiled shyly at me.

To my surprise the old man led me right to the far end of the longhouse, past another group of older women who were weaving mats from strips of split rattan and two who were weaving cloth on six-foot-long wooden frames. We clambered down the notched log and set off along a path shaded by the huge leaves of planted banana trees. Rounding a corner, we came to a group of huts, all built on stilts, like a longhouse in single sections. The old man climbed the notched pole into the first one and beckoned to me to do likewise.

It was dark inside; and the stench seemed to soak into me. A circle of people, presumably the old man's family, stood round an old woman, presumably his wife. She was sitting on a stool, a bundle of tied sticks in her hand, fanning her foot. As my eyes adjusted, I looked where everyone was looking: at her foot. My stomach turned again. The top surface was an open pool of fluid with a clearly-defined, raised shoreline of indented flesh. She moved slightly as she fanned herself and, as she did so, yellow and black and red islets of infection slithered gently to new positions on the watery surface of the wound. The sons and daughters looked at me, enquiringly. An earnest young man mimed someone entering the river and treading on—a fish. She had stepped on a fish-spine. Her sarong was pulled up to her waist and her leg was a dark reddish-brown right up to her thigh, about six inches above the knee.

She looked at me, her face resigned and dignified despite the pain, but her eyes big and brown and pleading. It was a terrible moment. She had, I supposed, gangrene. And she needed massive doses of penicillin, far more than we possessed. I gave her two tubes of Savlon, two packets of multivitamins, and a roll of bandages. In return, the old man gave me three sweet potatoes, which I took. It was the nastiest transaction of my life.

Distractedly, I walked off into the secondary jungle, the nearby land on its fifteen-year rest between crops, to be alone. A Spiderhunter called somewhere; and I thought I saw an Orange-bellied flower-pecker, a small burst of flame dancing from bush to bush. I sat down, halfway up the hill, in sight of the longhouse, beside some kind of large, purple-flowering orchid. Ought we to forget the Tiban range and take the woman to hospital in Kapit, a river's-length away? What ought we to do? So this was how the people of the far interior died—exactly as we had been told—of septicaemia, of one misjudged cut with a parang in a clearing, of a scratched mosquito-bite that became a boil, of a fish-spine in the foot. No wonder the population was so perpetually young, so beautiful. Perhaps Lubbock had got it the wrong way round in his *Prehistoric Times*. Perhaps it was not so much the "horrible dread of unknown evil" which "hangs like a cloud over savage life, and embitters every pleasure" but the very sensible dread, in this climate, of every passing accident, of every present micro-organism. They were certainly very stable societies, but perhaps this was exactly why they were so stable. The Niah caves excavations have revealed that the Borneo peoples of the true Stone Age ate the same kind of animals and made the same kind of boats as their probable descendants do today; and that the large mother-of-pearl fastenings on the ceremonial belts of Dana's daughters in the longhouse at Kapit are exactly the same as those worn by their ancestors forty thousand years ago.

When I got back to the longhouse James and the Iban were eating a lunch of rice and fish. I gave them the sweet potatoes; and I shared the problem with them.

"She dying," said Leon, "everyone know."

"But what would happen if we weren't here? Could she get to hospital? Ought we to take her downriver?"

"She very poor. Very poor. All those peoples there just come from Mahakam. They not yet in the longhouse. She have no money for petrols to come back from hospital. She not want to go. She never left her families in all her life; and hospital very, very far. Very difficult. She die soons."

"But what about the flying doctors?" said James. "What about a helicopter?"

"Too long, very too far for helicopter. These people never see a helicopter. Too far for flying."

Dana shrugged his shoulders and rolled himself a cheroot with Kenyah tobacco and a banana leaf. He spoke to Leon.

"The Tuai Rumah says we can take her to hospital on the way backs, if you want."

The Iban had helped us to evade the issue, to cease being troubled. We sat and smoked in silence. Dana laid aside his native cone of strong king-size Kenyah and helped himself to James's Gold Leaf.

"The Tuai Rumah says the river too low to travel," said Leon, "but we make the water rise tonight. He know the customs. He very powerful man."

Dana smiled his great chiefly smile, and waggled his finger at us, conspiratorially.

"We not to tell the Kenyah peoples because they harvest the padi. If they know we make our magics, they make their magics. They not want the rain."

Inghai grinned. It was an Iban plot.

"They not have guns," said Leon. "They want to take our guns for tomorrow. Poof poof to shoot the deer. We say no, absolute noes—you hurt yourselves. They angry with the Tuai Rumah, just a littles."

"Hang on," said James, looking worried and making a characteristically emphatic gesture—both arms out, his palms up and horizontal. "We do *not* want to upset these people. They're our hosts."

"I know, I know," said Leon, "but the Rumah will raise the river and then we leave and then they not our hosts."

A Kenyah woman came into the room, holding a necklace. She sat down beside us, and proffered the necklace to James.

"She want to sell it," said Leon.

"What does she want the money for?" asked James.

"To send downstream with her husband, after the harvest, when the mens go to trade with the Chinese peoples."

We inspected it in turn. It occurred to me that of all the presents we should have brought for the inland peoples, better than the aginomoto (the monosodium glutamate they all asked for), the sarongs, the salt, the cartridges, the batteries for their unused cassette player, the parang-blades from Kapit market, the ones they would have valued the most were the very objects which had seemed to us to be so obvious a nineteenth-century offering as to verge on the insulting: beads.

Beads, like the small brass gongs and the Chinese storage jars as big as a squatting-man (some of which date back to the Ming dynasty) to be found in almost every longhouse, are still a currency in Borneo. A few, made from shell and agate, were produced in the island; but most were imported by Arab and Chinese traders, some probably of Chinese manufacture, others from the Far East, and a few, almost certainly, from Venice. The most valuable of them all, the lukut sekala, a round black bead with delicate white and orange markings, used to be worth one healthy adult male slave, and would now cost well over a thousand pounds.

The bulk of this necklace was composed of yellow beads, labang, each one of which had been ground flat on the two surfaces that adjoined its neighbours by being fixed in the cut end of a piece of sugar-cane and rubbed against a smooth stone, probably about a hundred and fifty years ago. There were similar blue beads and seven much larger barrel-beads, black lukut, crudely painted with white, red and green stripes. The centre-piece was a pair of imitation pig-tusks, bound together with cloth, and fashioned from aluminium.

"Hey Redmond, I really want this," said James, running the necklace through his fingers.

"We get it for you, my very good friend," said Leon. "Our Tuai Rumah will talk to their second chief and he will talk to the woman and you will get the necklace. We bargains."

Dana and the woman went off to negotiate. James sat with his book, awaiting a conclusion of sale; Inghai crept into a corner, curled up, and went to sleep.

"Come on Redmon," said Leon, "now we find place for magics."

We climbed down the notched pole, made our way past the padi stores, and out along the river bank.

"We need a space to spin a pot," said Leon.

"Spin a pot?"

"Yes Redmon. We show you. Our Tuai Rumah—he knows all the customs."

"And you know a custom or two yourself, don't you Leon?"

"Sorries?"

"That girl in the pink sarong. She came to see you last night."

Leon grinned and took his Homberg hat off.

"You very dirty mans," he said, delighted.

"Leon, do you have a palang?"

"Who told you that word? How you know that word?" said Leon, genuinely startled.

"I read about it. I found it in a book."

"Ah," said Leon, "you and Jams, you not ordinary mens. Jams always reading books."

"He reads about palangs," I said, grinning myself.

"Huh!" said Leon, pointing a muscly finger in my face. "There's no need for you to smiles at the Iban. We know what you use."

"What do you mean?" I said, standing still with surprise.

Leon paused and looked about us theatrically, checking the undergrowth for spies, glancing up lest there be eavesdroppers in the coconut palm.

"You," said Leon, with great emphasis, "use goat's eyelashes."

"Good lord!" I said.

"I thought so!" said Leon, mightily pleased.

"But Leon, when do you have it done? When do you have the hole bored through your dick?"

"When you twenty-five. When you no good any more. When you too old. When your wife she feds up with you. Then you go down to the river very early in the mornings and you sit in it until your spear is smalls. The tattoo man he comes and pushes a nail through your spear, round and round. And then you put a pin there, a pin from the outboard-motor. Sometimes you get a big spots, very painfuls, a boil. And then you die."

"Jesus!"

"My best friend—you must be very careful. You must go down to the river and sit in it once a month until your spear so cold you can't feel it; and then you loosen the pin and push it in and out; or it will stick in your spear and you never move it and it makes a pebble with your water and you die."

"But Leon," I said, holding my knees together and holding my shock with my right hand, "do you have one?"

"I far too young!" said Leon, much annoyed; and then, grinning his broad Iban grin as a thought discharged itself: "But you need one Redmon! And Jams—he so old and serious; he need two!"

Leon bounded away down the path, roaring with laughter and scattering a stray flock of hens into the bushes.

I caught up with him beyond the banana plantation. He was standing on the beach of a steep-sided small lagoon. "Here we make our magics," announced Leon. "Now we tell the Tuai Rumah."

We collected Dana, James and Inghai from the longhouse and took them to the witching grounds. Inghai carried a basket. James looked even more chiefly than usual, his new charm of beads and metal pig tusks laurelled round his neck. I thought, as I fingered my own secret fetish in my pocket, a silver ankh given to me by my wife and all the other beautiful girls in her dress-making company in Oxford, of Edward B. Tylor's 1871 warning in *Primitive Culture*: "In our own time, West Africa is still a world of fetishes . . . Thus the one-sided logic of the barbarian, making the most of all that fits and glossing over all that fails, has shaped a universal fetish-philosophy of the events of life. So strong is the pervading influence, that the European in Africa is apt to catch it from the negro . . . Thus even yet some traveller, watching a white companion asleep, may catch a glimpse of some claw or bone or such-like sorcerer's trash secretly fastened round his neck." Still, if there was the very slightest chance that it would help us reach the headwaters of the Baleh and climb Mount Tiban with those terrible Bergens on our backs I was prepared to secrete anything that was not a worm or a bacillus or a virus or a python. In fact I would have settled for a totem pole, say, between my legs, or even a crucifix round my neck.

Inghai set down his basket and drew back the cover with his left hand, wiping his nose very slowly with the fingers of his right hand as he did so, a habit he indulged whenever he felt serious. The basket disclosed a wok, a packet of salt and a tortoise. Dana took out the wok and the packet and placed them on the shingle; he then leaped up the bank, drew his parang and cut down the branch of a palm tree.

Carrying his palm like a bishop's crosier, Dana indicated that we should do as he did. In a line parallel to the river we advanced to the wet stones, executed an about-turn and then marched ten paces back up the beach. Dana took a pinch of salt from the packet and buried it beneath a rock. We advanced back to the edge of the swirling river. Dana raised his palm branch, began a rhythmic Iban chant, and beat the water in time with his song. A much-startled Black-capped kingfisher, hawking insects from a perch on a dead tree to our right, dropped the dragonfly he was carrying and streaked off upriver, bright red and blue and yellow and disappearing fast.

"Good lucks!" said Leon. "He go up; we go up."

Dana waded into the water, chanting softly as he went, beating the river before him. Bending down, he planted the palm branch between the stones of the river bed, leaving about four feet of frond above the surface, where it fanned over, bent and trembling in the current.

"In the mornings," said Leon, "the river cover the palm."

"Our Tuai Rumah," said Inghai, deeply moved and bursting into speech, "we very lucks. He know the adat lama [the Iban laws and customs]. He great man."

Dana shouted to Inghai who then ran up the shingle, collected the wok and the comatose tortoise, took them out to the Lord of the House and returned to take up his position in the line.

Dana placed the tortoise in the wok and the wok on the concentric rings of a small eddy, mumbling very fast to himself as he did so and, with both hands, spinning wok and tortoise seven times to his left and seven times to his right.

"Hang on," said Leon with great earnestness, in a turn of speech caught from James, "now you say your England magics."

"Inglang magics! Jams! Inglang magics!" danced Inghai, much excited.

James paused and then rolled his enormous eyes backwards into his bald head until only the whites were visible. It was horrible to look upon. Leon and Inghai studied their toes on the pebbles, uneasily.

"On your feet, young river," intoned James, readjusting his corneas. "We goad you on the bum with palms. We tempt you with salt, like the salt in the sea. We raise you up to the air, as a tortoise breaks to the surface."

"Steady on, James," I said, unnerved, "we'll have an eighty-foot flood on our hands."

We hurried back to the longhouse. Dana, in addition to all his other abilities, was an accomplished meteorologist. Huge clouds were beginning to stack themselves in the east.

We finished the monitor lizard and some sebarau that Inghai had smoked, and then began to pack our Bergens for the journey in the morning. The chief's younger sons wandered in and out, themselves preparing for the trip to their outlying padi fields on the following day.

I sorted the disarranged contents of all my watertight plastic bags, took my malaria pills, counted the morphine syrettes just in case Dana or James had been injecting themselves in order to sleep through Leon's antics, and, when James was not looking, I practised my subcutaneous perforation technique on a lone banana. As I pushed down the plunger on my water-filled spare syringe, stuck in the fruit, a jet of liquid hissed out the other side and shot across the room. I resolved, in the event, to inject James in a buttock rather than an arm.

Sealing up the medical kit and placing it in the middle of the Bergen, well padded with socks, I sat down by the central tallow lamp as night came down, and began to look again with delighted disbelief at all the montane and submontane species which Smythies illustrates in *The Birds of Borneo*. The resident old woman, stopping her weaving of small pieces of fishing net, came and squatted down beside me on her haunches. I turned over the plates, very slowly. She bent forward, intrigued, and her distended, looped earlobes, weighted with some twenty brass rings apiece, cast two ellipses of shadow across the rough planks of the floor. It seemed to take her some time to realise that the pictures were images of birds, birds that she knew; and then she uncurled a thin arm from around herself and pointed with a creaky finger on which all the joints were swollen. It was Plate III, the Borneo raptors, and she pointed at the Brahminy kite, *Haliastur indus intermedius*. Tentatively, she stroked its red-brown back; and then she turned, her old eyes alight, and she smiled at me with one set of lips and one set of gums.

The Kenyah chief's two sons walked over to us and one or two men came in from the verandah. I continued to turn the pages. They nodded with recognition and pleasure and talked excitedly to each other; but there were obviously some matters of weighty dispute. James and Dana and Leon and Inghai joined us, and everyone sat down in a circle.

"Bejampong," said Leon firmly, putting his finger on the Crested jay, *Platylophus galericulatus coronatus*, a brown perky bird with a white crescent at the back of its neck and a plume like a second tail growing out of the back of its head. "He very cheeky, like Inghai. And he talk a lots, like me."

"Wass that?" said Inghai, sleepily, giving Leon a push.

"Very important bird for we Iban," said Leon. "He sing like hot sticks. We must hear him, after we chop the trees but before we burn the hills, to plant the padi."

Leon mimed the fire with his fingers flickering like flames and made a rapid, crackling cry. The Kenyah nodded.

"See," said Leon, taking the book, "they agrees with me. And you must hear the bejampong before you goes hunting or for fights. He very quicks; you be very quicks. And his jugu"—Leon pointed at the jay's crest—"is like the hair on the head of a man you don't like"—Leon held up a patch of his own hair with his free hand—"and so you will take heads."

There was an awkward silence, and Leon, realising that he had got over-excited and spoken out of turn, sheepishly handed *The Birds of Borneo* to his Tuai Rumah. Headmaster Dana proceeded to turn the pages with an air of authority, lecturing James and me, in official tones, in Iban.

"He the Tuai Burong," said Leon, "he know what the birds tell to us. Very, very difficults for ordinary mens. He dream dreams for chiefs. Not like our very naughties dreams, absolute no. Singalang Burong invite him to his house in the sky, to meet the birds, his—how do you say?—the husbands of his daughters. They called keptupong, embuas, beragai, papau, bejampong, pangkas and nendak. They look after we Iban. They speak to us and our Tuai Burong he understand."

Dana held the book open for all to see, his thumb on the *Diard's trogon*, a long-tailed thrush-like bird with a black chest and a scarlet stomach, a fairly common but rarely seen resident of primary jungle up to about 4,000 feet.

"Pau, pau, pau, pau, pau, pau," sang Dana in an ascending scale. "He make the sound," said Leon. "Very good lucks sound this bird. Beragai laki and Beragai indu, the man and the wife in a bush. You can't see them. They laughs. You have good hunting; and then you laughs, too."

Dana rifled through the plates and found a pair of Banded kingfishers, the male banded blue and black, the female black and brown, primitive tree-living deep-jungle kingfishers who are never seen over water.

"Pi-pit, pi-pit, pi-pit," sang Dana, in falsetto.

"Very bad lucks," said Leon, unknowingly disagreeing with Freeman's anthropological opinion that the Banded kingfisher is baka orang mentas jako, like someone speaking kindly. "Embuas laki and Embuas indu—you hear them, you turn back, or you harms. If they fly mimpin, from your rights to your left, you runs back, all the way."

At that moment there was a distant crack of thunder; rain began to fall on the roof, way up above the great dim rafters, up above the feeble shadows cast by the lamp.

"Badas!" said Dana, with an enormous grin, forgetting himself and flexing both his champion biceps.

Inghai beamed with pride, and then looked with awe at his hero, the Lord of the House, the Bringer of the Rains.

"Our Tuai Rumah, he the best chief in all Kapit," said Leon.

"Clever old Rumah zoomer," whispered James, "but I think he's been systematically pinching my ciggies."

Seeing that the Kenyah were about to leave us and the party break up, I quickly dug Lord Medway's *Mammals of Borneo* out of my Bergen and opened it at a photograph of *Didermocerus sumatrensis harrissoni*, the Borneo (Sumatran or Asiatic) two-horned rhinoceros.

"Leon, ask them if they've ever seen this."

Leon touched his eyes and then pointed at the picture, a captive female from Sumatra wallowing in her private mud pool in the Botanic Gardens (Kebun Raya), Bogor, Indonesia.

There was much shaking of heads.

"Everyone heard tell of it," said Leon, "even at Kapit; but no one ever seen it."

So then I tried them on a rare bird, confined to Borneo, the Bald-headed woodshrike, *Pityriasis gymnocephala*, for which Ernst Mayr, at the Museum of Comparative Zoology at Harvard, had asked us to search. "The birds are slow and heavy in movements," writes Smythies, "keep to the middle canopy, and are difficult to frighten"; it had crossed my mind that the best way to observe them might well be to leave James out in a clearing and wait for them to come down to mate.

The grey-backed, red-throated, big-billed and bald-headed bird sat on its perch on Plate XLV (just below another Borneo rarity, the Great tit) and looked lugubriously at the assembled company through its little black eye. There was no answering look of recognition. No one had seen it; no one had heard of it.

Disappointed, I put my books away, and everyone went to bed. As the rain beat steadily on the atap roof I stayed awake, reading my Notebook of Useful Hints for life in the jungle, in the Mount Batu Tiban section under the sub-heading *Leeches*. In Oxford I had abstracted a paper by Smythies in the *Sarawak Museum Journal* for July–December 1957, but the whole subject now seemed less academic. Quoting Harding and Moore's great work on *Hirudinea* Smythies remarks that "Very little relating to the leeches of Borneo has been published and our knowledge of them remains meagre. Undoubtedly many species await discovery and description. They are to be sought as external parasites on fishes, batrachians, turtles, crocodiles, and aquatic birds, in the air passages of water-frequenting mammals, etc., and burrowing forms under logs and in the humus of the rain forests. The true land and tree leeches will present themselves without being sought . . ." The Borneo land leeches belong to the family *Hirudinea*, "the Ten-eyed blood-sucking leeches"; and a "leech that appears linear when extended may be egg-shaped in complete contraction. When unfed and resting it may be greatly flattened, transparent, pale-coloured and rough, with protruded, alert, sensory pappillae, and when gorged with blood the same leech will be many times larger, distended, thick, opaque, dark-coloured and smooth."

And one must be careful when drinking from rivulets in mountain jungle, because of the Thread leech which attacks the nose and mouth: "The presence of this leech is usually advertised by bleeding from the nose, and various Dusuns reported having seen wild animals, such as rats and mousedeer, infested by small leeches . . . They are local in distribution and apparently confined to clean mountain streams . . . The danger of this leech lies in its being very inconspicuous and having an exceptional reach for its size; it stretches to a thread.

The Dusuns almost invariably assemble a spout made of a cleft of bamboo or of leaves when they require to drink from streams . . ." But all that was as nothing when compared with the Giant leech: "John Whitehead (*The Exploration of Mt Kinabalu*, p 165) writes: 'Tungal brought in an enormous leech; when it reared itself up it was quite a foot long of a pale cream colour. He found this horrible creature in the pathway close to the camp . . .' Audy and Harrison (1952:2) also found leeches of this type on Kinabalu: 'Two distinctive and very large leeches were also encountered. One giant pallid leech came from the bridle-path near Tinompok. The other, darker and smaller, came from Kambarongah at 7,500 feet.'" And, most disturbing of all: "Dr. Nieuwenhuis (SMJ 1956, VII, 7 : 123) mentions native reports of giant leeches on Mt Batu Tiban."

Should I tell James? Or would it be kinder simply to allow him to pull them out of his pants when the need arose?

Whilst debating this difficult matter with myself, I became aware of a small figure at the far end of the room. It was Leon's girl in the pink sarong. Her step was delicate, her body sinuous, her movements quick and light. She hesitated when she saw my torch, so I switched it off and lay down. She reached Leon safely, without discovery, and soon their happy giggles and whispers mingled with the now-gentle sound of rain on the roof.

I fell asleep and dreamed of Leon and his beautiful young girl; of palangs and two foot leeches; and of Harrison's leeches who "when they sense the presence of a victim . . . stand up stiffly on the hinder sucker with the straight rigid body at an angle to the vertical".

TEN

At dawn I hurried down to the witching ground. The palm frond had disappeared; and the water had risen to a new shore-line, just beneath the stone that covered the beguiling pinch of salt. I helped it on its way with a splash or two and then took a swim in the men's bathing area, where I was well groomed by catfish.

Lower down, the bank was crowded with small canoes. Families were embarking to begin the short journey up or down river to their outlying farms. The men stood up and poled from the back; the women sat in the bows beneath their enormous round hats, paddling; and the children, sitting in the middle, held a puppy with one hand and a picture of the Queen with the other.

The dogs were much agitated. Gathered in a pack on the shore, they yelped and howled, anxiously jostling for position and eyeing their own favourite family, ready to jump and yowl from boulder to boulder, alongside the struggling canoes, until all was right with the world again and they were re-united on the padi fields.

Dana supervised the loading of our boat, the stowing of the newly bought rice supply, and Inghai's lashing of the tarpaulins. Leon attended to the outboard motor, revving it up and then cocking it out of the water to impress a group of girls on the bank. We snatched a breakfast of fish pieces and said solemn goodbyes to our hosts.

Leon set and started the motor in earnest and we swung out into the middle of the river, passing the fleet of Kenyah canoes that were hugging the bank. Leon's girl in the pink sarong stood on a little knoll above the landing beach, waving to her disappearing lover; and Leon, looking back every few yards, cursed in Iban by Dana and Inghai, zigzagged the boat wildly until we were out of sight.

For the first miles the hills were covered in secondary jungle, or this year's padi fields, the blackened stumps of felled and burned giant forest trees rising a few feet above the crop. But gradually the

Kenyah fields, with their accompanying temporary huts on stilts, became less frequent; and the primary jungle reasserted itself. We passed a tree in flower, a burst of red spikes in the unending, multitudinously various shades of green. Scattered across the square miles of jungle all the individuals of that particular species would be extending their scarlet invitation to a nectar-drinking party for sun-birds, and so effecting their own pollination. Yet in a land with no proper seasons and where each species of tree holds its own spring — every eight or ten or fourteen months, according to its primordial fancy — the butterflies and airborne beetles and moths and sunbirds and bats (on pale-looking, foetid-smelling, night-opening flowers) may drink nectar all year long and every tree is almost certain to be fertilised; but there is never a great canopy of different colours, no united blaze of spring blossom to be seen in the jungle.

Huge oaks and chestnuts crowded down to the water. Their branches, hung and looped and dangled with lianas, reached out over the river edges and hid the banks, so that we seemed to be twist-ing and turning, rising, climbing slowly into a mountain interior along a stretch of water that ran endlessly through the forest on either side. The balance of species appeared to have changed; but knowing that in any one ten-hectare plot of Borneo jungle there may be up to eight hundred different kinds of tree, I gave up trying to identify them. We were, after all, travelling in one of the oldest and richest and most stable environments on earth, where every species had had ample time to change its evolutionary course as often and as tortuously as the convoluted wanderings of the creepers all about us.

Lesser fish-eagles, Little green herons, Stork-billed and Black-capped kingfishers reappeared, in greater numbers than before. The river grew still narrower, the great trees almost touching overhead, and the water itself became clear. As Leon edged the canoe carefully across the pools above each rapid, we peered over the side of the hollowed tree trunk, and watched the shoals of black and silver fish hanging in the current. Big, bright red dragonflies quartered the surface.

We entered a small, straight stretch of river split in two by a bank of shingle.

"Look at that! Quick!" said James, pointing ahead.

"Sentuku! Sentuku!" shouted Dana.

A pair of huge, black-winged birds were flying, one behind the other, across the river, their long plumed tail feathers dazzling white in the sun: the rare White-crested hornbill, *Berenicornis comatus*.

"Badas!" said Dana, and gave orders to Leon.

"Now we make a food," said Leon, running the boat gently up on the shingle.

Dana and Inghai collected driftwood, chopped it to length with their parangs, and made a fire to boil the rice and fish. Leon disappeared with his harpoon beneath the overhanging trees along the bank; and James and I stripped to our y-fronts and went for a swim. In the bright, clear water swarms of tiny fish surrounded us; a watery kaleidoscope of red and gold and silver flashed around our legs as they turned and wheeled and darted, chasing the flecks of soap. James stood there in the jungle river, slowly lathering a block of Palmolive between his cupped hands, dropping globules of froth into the water, entranced, collecting droves of fish about his knees.

"Jams! Makai!" shouted Inghai at last, holding up a mess-tin.

"Oh God," said James, waking from his moment of happiness, "how I could do with a decent meal."

As we sat on our various boulders, protected from the midday sun by hats and towels, gingerly sucking sebarau flesh from its tufts of bones, a group of extraordinary birds arrived over the pool in front of us. They were obviously swifts, but they were huge, their bodies as big as starlings, and they hurtled over the water like grotesque swallows, their scimitar-shaped wings rattling and creaking with effort as they dipped their beaks with a splash into the water and then flew round to repeat the process, hawking insects as they went.

"Who the hell are those guys?" said James.

"Hang on," I said (we had all caught the poet's speech patterns) "I'll have a lookette in Smythies."

The birds were unconcerned as I went to the dugout and took Smythies and the binoculars out of my Bergen. They seemed to be swearing at each other, a high-pitched *sheeeet*, but a series of drum beats as they made their water-approach must have been coming from their wings.

"They're obviously *ur*-swifts," said James. "A lousy prototype with the aerodynamics all wrong, since discarded by the Benevolent Creator."

"There's no need to be provocative, just because you can't eat your sebarau."

"God, it's *awful*," said James, putting his mess-tin down in disgust on the shingle, where it immediately filled up with butterflies.

Smythies soon put us right: they were Brown spinetailed swifts, *Hirundapus giganteus*. Amidst the great press of unseen birds, the bewildering variety of clear calls and background chatter from the jungled banks of the river, it was again absurdly satisfying to have put a name to something, to have given its image firm and marked brain space, to have taken possession of *Hirundapus giganteus* and stored its flight in memory, to know that it was "Resident in Borneo in small numbers" and that Smythies, too, thought that "on the wing it has a queer heavy look". I picked up the binoculars to check out its supposed "white under tail-coverts" but it was no use: the unprotected Nikons were now opaque, a mass of fungus had finally grown right across the lenses, deep inside the tubes.

Leon gutted, chopped up and salted away two sebarau that he had caught, throwing their bleeding heads into the shallows where they at once became two writhing silver balls of little fish. We then set off again up the narrowing river. The rapids were almost continuous, but the volume of water was now too small to be ferocious.

High up, a pair of Black eagles seemed to be keeping lazy watch over our slow progress, sailing round and round above the bright little thread of river lost in the jungle. Leaf monkeys, too, accompanied us, troops of them rustling and crashing about in the trees at the water's edge, peering out, for a second or two, as we passed.

We spent most of the afternoon with the outboard motor switched off, tilted and silent on its frame as we dragged the dugout up the rapids, with nothing to disturb the constant noise of the jungle but the sound of broken water amongst the rocks and Dana's shout from the bow: "Saytu, dua, tiga—bata!" We stopped frequently to rest and to look at the ever-closing jungle, and perhaps that is why we noticed, for the first time, a tiny kingfisher, a flash of yellow which whistled as it flew, the Rufous-backed kingfisher, a robin-sized dart of energy beneath the overhanging trees.

At about four o'clock Dana began to look for a place to camp, but the vegetation was far too thick, the trees and bushes crowded together, pressing out over the water to gather the direct and the reflected sunlight. And then, as we pulled the canoe round a bend awkwardly studded with small boulders, we stopped and we stared in excited disbelief. Ahead, the Baleh divided into two. To our left the Balang, to our right the Upper Baleh, burbled together and swirled into a deep pool. Past floods had cut deep terraces into the banks, about fifteen feet above the river surface, where as yet nothing but short saplings had established themselves. The pool itself was ringed with ochre-coloured shingle, edged with boulders and driftwood. So here was the last divide on the Baleh—a place I had looked at often and longingly on the map but which I had secretly thought would be out of reach. It was an enclosed, still world of gentle water: Brown spinetailed swifts, the fattest swifts alive, were circling the pool, diving down, puckering its surface into splashes with their beaks, and heaving themselves back into the air.

"Badas! Badas!" shouted Dana, raising one tattooed fist and bunching up a bicep as if he had made the place himself.

"Now we *really* catch some fish," said Leon.

"Oh God," said James.

"And there some vegetables," said Leon as we approached the bank.

"Where?" said James, brightening absurdly, as if he expected a pile of parsnips to be awaiting his arrival in this hallowed place.

"There," said Leon, pointing with one arm as he steered the dugout to shore with the other, "on the bushes. Peas." It was a straggly thicket, covered with dark green berries.

"Terong pipit," said Dana, adding something in Iban with great vehemence.

"The Tuai Rumah, he say they taste like little shits," said Leon, grinning.

"Rat shit! Rat shit!" called look-out Inghai, unexpectedly, from the bow.

"Rat shit or not," said James decisively, "I'm going to have some. I can't stick this rice and fish much longer."

"Don't you worry," said Leon, looking concerned, "my very best friend, soon you be all right. Soon we make fish soups."

James took the mess-tins and began collecting terong pipit. Inghai gathered driftwood, and Leon and Dana, having secured the dugout to two giant trees with long lengths of our parachute cord, set about clearing a patch of jungle for our base camp hut. I spread my soaking, river-slimy shirt and trousers and socks out to dry on a boulder and sat back to watch the butterflies arrive. They came, flapping and gliding, undulating, half-looping or flying straight and fast, from the bushes, the shingle, from beneath the trees; and some, it seemed, just appeared fully-formed out of the empty air. There were the usual

Rajah Brooke's birdwings, Yellows and Blues and Swallow-tails, but more members, I thought, of the *Danaidae* family, of the large, dark-coloured butterflies whose black or brown wings were streaked on both their surfaces with an iridescent blue or green, or spotted and striped with white and yellow. They were so tame that Inghai, small and quick as a mongoose, could pick them up by their closed wings as they fed. Somehow storing in their bodies residues of the poisonous plants on which they feed as caterpillars, all these butterflies seemed to flaunt themselves, unafraid of predators. They had settled on James, I noticed, sucking the sweat from his back as he toiled over his berry-picking.

I put on my now merely damp, hot clothes, and climbed up the bank to help Dana and Leon build our hut. They had made a clearing between some large chestnuts and were cutting and trimming four stout saplings into posts, sharpening one end of each with deft, powerful swipes of their parangs. We used one post as a pile-driver to make four deep holes in the soft soil at each corner of a fifteen foot square. Inserting the uprights, the rudimentary plan of an outsize four-poster began to emerge. We set cross-pieces some two feet above the ground and lashed them to the poles with lengths of rattan creeper, hauled down from a tree and cut into strips by Leon. On this framework we laid smaller, springy saplings, a mattress-floor; and then we added a sloping roof of latticed branches. Finally, Inghai, the junior, was summoned from his fires and his own newly-built smoking-house to go off into the jungle and collect the right kind of leaves, one set to make the canopy and one to act as our bottom sheet.

Dana, surveying his labours, looked about him with obvious satisfaction. He then sat down on the edge of the floor, rummaged about in his private chiefly basket, a woven bag of dyed split rattan worked into a design of dancing figures, and, to my surprise, drew out the pipe and the tin of Balkan Sobranie with which I had presented him in Kapit. He laid them beside him on the poles, leaned forward to where I was sitting, shook my hand, and then, with a dazzling grin, the sun lighting his three gold front teeth, he stood up and saluted. I jumped to my feet, snapped to attention on the leaf litter, and, immensely pleased, returned the compliment. Leon clapped. Dana, I reflected, knew all about decorum: his ferociously democratic people had certainly elected the right man chief.

"He know your customs too," said Leon, proudly. "He very

happies. The Tuai Rumah—he think we never reach this far place. Very far."

"Why not? Because of the rapids?"

"No, my best friend—because Jams so old and you so fats." Leon roared with laughter. "Jams! Jams!" he shouted, holding up the arak can. "Now we celebrates! Now we have a party!"

James climbed carefully up the bank, clutching two mess-tins piled high with terong pipit.

"And we eat fish soups and we eat Jams's little shits!" Leon concluded, filling up our mugs with arak.

Inghai returned with a huge bundle of palm leaves which he spread on the pole floor of the hut and then, after much discussion in Iban, he helped Dana and Leon spread the canoe tarpaulins over the roof. It certainly was a snug room with a view, a view out across the darkening pool above which two Eared nightjars were already hunting. As I watched them flickering back and forth across the tops of the trees on the opposite bank, I sipped my arak and remembered a passage from Shelford's *A Naturalist in Borneo* which I had transcribed into my notebook: "It is singular that in many parts of the world sinister habits are attributed to the Night-jar. In England the bird has been accused of sucking udders of cattle and goats, as its alternative name, the Goat-sucker, signifies. The more Rabelaisian fancy of the Malay charges the bird with attacks on human beings, which for modesty's sake I dare not specify further."

As James put the finishing touches to his cooking fire he had as yet, I reflected, little idea of the pleasures in store for him.

Inghai, too, was preparing to cook. With unusual attention to his duties and perhaps inspired by the competition, he was sorting through the mess of salted fish in Dana's tin and assembling a row of secret ingredients in small bundles of wrapped cloth beside his bubbling cauldron. James, intent, rummaged in his Bergen. He drew out a mysterious, opaque plastic bag.

"Now then, Redmond," said James, "it is time you learned to cook. First, we survey the *batterie de cuisine*: Aunt Noel's nail scissors (for stalking terong pipit); Tom Sutcliffe's penknife; Dana's wok; Inghai's slice for frying; two SAS mess-tins."

James, tidy by temperament, laid out the instruments in single file on a tree root. Leon and Dana came to stand and look.

"And here," said James, opening his bag, "is my huge surprise."

It was a small clutch of onions and garlic.

"For every pound of terong pipit," intoned James, "take four shalots and four cloves of garlic. Slice. Heat oil in wok. Fry onion and garlic until golden brown. Add three generous penknife-bladefuls of curry powder. Wash the terong pipit which you have previously stalked and add to the wok. Take a generous sprinkling of coarse salt and three and a half penknife-bladefuls of aginomoto. Stir. Cover. Cook for fifteen minutes (or until the terong pipit are soft). Add lemon juice and serve immediately with boiled rice. Drink one gallon of arak."

Dana looked unimpressed. Leon nudged Inghai. Ominous chatter in Iban took place.

"We, too, have surprises," announced Leon. "Iban surprises."

The cooks withdrew to their separate stations. The nightjars disappeared. The fires grew brighter as the night grew darker. The wet air filled with the sound of bubbling pots and the vibrating membranes of thousands of cicadas.

Inghai huddled over his cauldron, stirring it with a stick. The cauldron itself appeared to be blowing blisters of bubble gum from its upturned mouth, chewing and steaming and puffing up fifty or sixty packets of white Wrigley's at each burp of its greasy lips.

"Fish soups, very specials for we Iban," said Leon, helpful as always. And then, with a passing twinge at the back of the throat, I remembered the rudiments of my fish biology lessons. The top of the pot was dancing with swim-bladders, with the internal balloons of the sebarau.

"Okay, gang," said James, expertly serving up a black mess into four tins and one mug, "we now have the pleasure to present the Fenton *hors d'oeuvre*."

James took up his spoon and began to eat. "Makai! Makai!" he said, pleased with himself.

Dana sniffed and looked about, concerned. Inghai laid his mug aside. Leon prodded his hot pile of terong pipit with a forefinger and licked its end, gingerly. James had that look that cooks get, that evident readiness to avenge an insult with disproportionate violence, so I tried a mouthful. They tasted a bit like school peas, or rather they tasted a bit like school peas might if you took each one and injected it with a small dose of that particular haemorrhoid cream which is made from the oil of shark's fins. A tiny movement, to my left, caught my eye. Dana's tattooed hand had made a quick flip towards a bush.

"Badas!" said Dana, wiping his lips, putting down his empty mess-tin. "Badas, Jams!"

"Just a squillionth part too rich, do you think?" said James.

"No, no. *Perfetto*, *ottime*. Vegetables at last, entirely thanks to you," I said, as the haemorrhoid cream squeezed itself between my teeth, flowed thick and viscous and warm beneath my tongue, oozed up to oil my epiglottis.

"Ouches! Ouches!" shouted Leon suddenly, jumping up from his seat on the jungle floor, clutching his buttocks, knocking his tin over, stamping the ground with his feet. "Ants! very bloody ants!"

"Never mind," said James, "there's a bit more here."

"No, noes, thank you," said Leon, rubbing his stomach, "badas. But now I full up."

Inghai gathered up the tins to wash in the river, and took his mugful of terong pipit with him.

"Soon we have fish soups," said Leon. "Very special dish for we Iban."

The swim bladders bounced wildly on the boiling liquid, glistening in the firelight.

Inghai returned with the clean tins and the empty mug and ladled out the broth and bubble gum. And then, at the bottom of my tin, I made a wonderful discovery. So this was the surprise: the Iban, all this time, had been keeping a present of spaghetti for us.

"James — it's spaghetti! Why didn't they tell us?"

"Er — perhaps not, strictly speaking. You try some. Take a really big mouthful, I should, or you won't catch that subtle flavour."

I wrapped a few lengths round my spoon. They certainly did not bend in that obliging way that spaghetti has. And the consistency was all wrong — a good, long, rubbery chew. I edged closer to the fire, scooped up a bundle of limp pieces from my tin and inspected them. Each section of spaghetti had a black tip at its end.

"You the running shits?" asked Leon, sympathetically, masticating well.

"Leon, what the hell are these things?"

"Very good," said Leon, "we save them in salts till we reach this far place. They the little snakes that live in the fishes. How you say it?"

"Jesus!" I said, "worms."

"Jesus worms," said Leon, "very good."

James edged gently out of the circle of firelight, towards a bush.

"And now," said Leon, "we have more party. We have smoke fish and rices and arak and then we find Ukit girl for Ingy-Pingy."

"Ukit girl?"

"Ukit girl very beautiful," said Leon. "We now in Ukit country. But we never see them. The Ukit they always see you before you see them. They the kings of the jungle. They best of all the peoples with the blowpipe. You never see—not even a leaf move. Phut! Phut! You die. You have five or ten minutes time for running, depending on how fats you are. Ingy-Pingy—he die in two minutes. Redmon— he die in half an hour."

Leon translated his witticisms, and Dana, amidst the Iban merriment, put down his plate of smoked fish and re-filled our mugs with arak.

"There was an Ukit once at Kapit," said Leon. "They captured him in the jungle and took him away to the police in Kapit and the government were going to send him to school." Leon paused theatrically, just so we would realise what a good story his lordship was about to tell us.

"And then what happened?" said James.

"The Ukit—he had his own language. He want to go back to his peoples in the jungle, far, far away. He not want to learn to speak like the Malay peoples. He not want to speak even like the Iban peoples. And he say he not going to school. And one day he sitting in Kapit, near the Iban market, on the wall by the corner where the wooden bridge is, with the policeman who guard him. All the policeman Malays, but they not take away the Ukit parang, the Ukit knife. The knife is very special to the Ukit. You not take it away."

"So?" said James.

"The Ukit stood up" (Leon bounded up and sideways) "and he cut the head off the policeman." Leon drew out his own parang and curled it through the air.

"Steady on," said James.

"And then the Ukit run like a deer. No one run as fast as an Ukit. He run up the hill and hide in a garden. And then all the policemen go and find him and bring him back and take away his knife and put him in a room where the policemen live. But the Ukit too quick. He too clever for them. He get out of his room and he jump the big fence. He jump seven feet, and he run and hide in the pond in Kapit. He hide down in the pond and breathe through a straw. So the policemen come with big sticks and they beat the water and they take the Ukit out again. And then they all go to Kuching with the Ukit."

"And what did they do to him?"

"I not know," said Leon, shrugging his shoulders. "They probably take his head off."

Inghai nodded his assent, clutching a mug full of arak. Dana seemed oblivious of our ethnographical discussion as, holding his pipe in his teeth, he covered himself with our insect repellent.

"And who are the Ukit?" I asked. "Are they like the Punan?"

"They more clever than the Punan," said Leon. "They the greatest hunters in all the world."

"Will we meet them? Could you find them?"

"We try," said Leon, "but they too clever. They know every tree in the jungle. They not like the water. They not fish like me. We Iban — we make boats and big houses and grow rices and fish with harpoon and the jala. But you not go to the Ukit house because the Ukit he not build a house. He sleep in the jungle like the wild pigs, like babi. Mens and womens and children all together. The Tuai Rumah say when an Ukit die they just leave him for the animals to eat — but we Iban we bury our fathers and they help us when we in trouble."

"How will they like it," said James, "when we walk right into their territory?"

Leon leaned over and took James by the arm.

"You be all right, my very best friend," said Leon, laughing. "I jokes. They very gentle peoples. They go away. They not disturb us."

"What do they eat?" said James.

"Roast babi," said Leon, longingly. "And monkeys and deers and squirrels and birds." Leon paused. "They eat a lot, Jams, my good friend. But no fishes and no rices."

"They know what they're doing," said James, "they've worked it out."

"And they take sago from the palm tree," said Leon, "and they change bits of tree, very smelly wood — how you say it? — for iron for knives and for making the blowpipe, the sumpitan, from the Kenyah and the Kayan peoples."

"Camphor," said James.

"Thassit," said Leon. "And the Ukit girls — the Tuai Rumah he say they very beautifuls. They not brown like us, more whiter like you. They very small, like Inghai."

"Ingy-Pingy, pudding and pie," said Inghai slowly, as if he had just worked out the implications of $E = Mc^2$ all by himself, "kiss the girls and make them cry."

"Look, you may be small," said James to Inghai, "but you're a good egg."

"Good egg," repeated Inghai, helping himself to more arak, "good egg."

"God, I could eat an egg now," said James, "couldn't you?"

"Yes, double egg, beans, chips, sausage and peas, with the fried egg all crinkly round the edges."

"You're so crude, Redmond. A Spanish omelette, that's what we need. In fact, I'll make you a promise: if we ever get out of here I'll make you a Spanish omelette; in my cool, comfortable, clean, spacious kitchen, entirely free of ants and mosquitoes and fish and snakes. I will cook you an omelette such as you never dreamed *Homo sapiens* would be capable of creating, and, after supper, your bloodstream entirely free of arak but saturated with Glenmorangie, you may pay a private visit to my best lavvy, whose bowl, as far as I know, *has never seen a catfish*. Anyway, where are all the eggs? The Kenyah longhouse was clucking with chickens. It was one three-hundred-yard-long all-in deep-litter shithouse for chickens. So where the hell are the eggs?"

"They must go to the spirits. We never saw anyone eating an egg. Perhaps they've got Bungan."

"Bungan?" said James. "It's certainly what I've got. I really can't face all that performance in the river. Melanie Klein's rich and fruitful offerings in the river flushroony. I shall just hole up for a week or two."

"No, no—it's a religion. I read about it in the *Sarawak Museum Journal*. It began about thirty years ago: some poor Kenyah called Jok Apoi had a rotten run of harvests and a wife and child and not enough rice to feed them with and he didn't know what to do. So like Kékulé with the benzene ring he very sensibly solved his problem with a dream: Bungan, a sexy Kenyah goddess, paid him a visit. 'Look here, Jok,' she said, 'if you want to grow a lot of rice you must work at it. It's no good downing tools every time a bird flies the wrong way or a deer calls. Forget all that and let me help you. If you're off to plant the padi or to go hunting, just take an egg, think of me, point it end-on in the direction you want to go, and then stick it in a tall split-bamboo egg-cup outside the longhouse. After that, you can ignore all the omens. Nothing can get you.'"

"And that did the trick?"

"Apparently it did. Everyone thought he'd gone ga-ga to begin with—but then his crops won all the local shows and Bungan was on in a big way."

"And they swiped all the eggs."

"Afraid so."

Inghai was stretched out fast asleep on the floor of the hut. Dana and Leon were preparing to go to bed, stamping out James's fire and piling wet logs on the other two.

"You'd believe anything," said James, hanging his mosquito net from the roof poles so that it draped down over his patch of palm leaf bedding.

I gave Leon and Dana and James their after-supper dose of vitamin C (half a gram), vitamin B and multivitamins, and a paracetomol each to Leon and Dana for their suddenly remembered headaches. I then secretly resumed my prophylactic course of antibiotics with a Strepto-triad, and, just in case the long, white, black-headed intestinal worms of the sebarau should reconstitute themselves in my own gut and attempt to make their escape to the river with a wriggle from my every orifice, I added a depth charge of codeine phosphate.

Dana sat close to the fire for a moment or two, his broken mirror clutched between his knees. Tweezers poised, he checked his face by the light of the flames for stray, emergent hairs, until, evidently satisfied that no such unsightliness had crept upon him unawares, he retired to bed. I got into my mosquito net and tucked its sides hard in under the strewn leaves. Behind the netting beside me, James was silhouetted by the light of his torch, propped up on his elbow, reading.

As I lay and listened, two feet off the jungle floor on the outer end of our verandah hut, I thought I could hear, above the background electrical-shorting noise of a million cicadas and the swirl of river water between a thousand small rocks, disparate rustlings. Yes—something mouse-size was moving and sniffing where James had jettisoned his fish soups; and the leaves were being scuffed round and about where Leon had kicked over his terong pipit. Surely, I reasoned to myself, full of excitement and arak in equal proportions, only one animal in all Borneo would be a match for James's terong pipit. It could only be *Gymnurus albus*, the Borneo subspecies of the stinking shrew, the rabbit-sized bundle of a nocturnal pong so bad that pigs reverse into pig wallows whenever he appears, leopard-cats put their paws across their noses and fall out of trees and snakes stick their heads up their arses. Almost completely white bar its naked rat-like tail, as conspicuous as it is possible to be in the night-time jungle short of a covering of phosphorescence, *Gymnurus albus*, the Moonrat, skunks about with relative impunity. But no—the circumambient smell in the humid air was no worse than usual, the sweet odour of rot with a tang of sweat was probably the fragrance of the waste products of numberless colonies of bacteria feeding upon myself, rather than the actively manufactured Offensive Protection of a gymnure, and there was no hairy patch of white hedgehogging round the fire. So I settled down to my notebook.

Snakes, like leeches, I decided, had now become a subject of peculiar interest. My Useful Hints no longer seemed quite so funny. There are two species of python in Borneo, *Python reticulatus* and *Python curtus*. *Python reticulatus* is by far the largest, and by far the most common. "The colouring," as Shelford observes *en passant*, "strikes a visitor to a museum as highly conspicuous, but as a matter of fact the snake in its natural haunts in jungle is difficult to see." I found this easy to believe. "It is occasionally found coiled up amongst the roots of some forest giant, but when on the look-out for a meal is said to hang head downwards along the trunk of a tree with its tail coiled round a branch . . ."

And then Shelford quotes the following from the *Sarawak Gazette* of April 1981, p 52:

At Judan, a village some six miles from Muka, a man and his son, aged from 10 to 12 years, were sleeping in their house, inside a mosquito curtain. They were on the floor near the wall. In the middle of the night, the father was awakened by his son calling out, the lamp was out and the father passed his hand over his son but found nothing amiss, so he turned over and went to sleep again, thinking the boy was dreaming. Shortly afterwards the child again called out saying that a crocodile was taking him. This time the father, thoroughly aroused, felt again and found that a snake had closed his jaws on the boy's head; he then prized open the reptile's mouth and released the head of his son, but the beast drew the whole of his body into the house and encircled the body of the father; he was rescued by the neighbours who were attracted by the cries for help of the terrified couple. The snake when killed was found to be about 15 feet long. The head and forehead of the boy are encircled with punctured wounds produced by the python's teeth.

Comforting myself with the thought that any discriminating python, given the chance, would avoid the unpleasant tickle of hair in the throat and go for a trouble-free first-time gulp, a bald initial bolus, I nevertheless wished that we were more than two feet above the python pavement—thirty-two feet say, would have done, or full python length plus two.

ELEVEN

I awoke in the dark, itching horribly. I switched on my torch and searched the interior of my mosquito net: nothing. And there were no tears in the fabric. It was an all-over itch, a kind of nettle-rash and cat-flea bite combined. I turned the torchlight on my bare arm. It was pepper-dusted with moving dots. The palm leaves were swarming with tiny black bugs.

Deciding that they could hardly be lice specially adapted for attachment to the fine hairs of *Homo sapiens*, I stripped off fast, covered myself in a slimy mixture of Anthisan (anti-itch) and Autan (anti-louse) and squelched back into my dry clothes.

James began to move. There was a sighing and a swearing from inside his mosquito net.

"Itching?" I asked. "Pox?"

James's bald head emerged from his net and wandered eight inches into the night, white as a gymnure.

"Something," he announced, thoughtfully, "has been taking a snackette on my bum."

I handed him the tubes of Autan and Anthisan and fetched our hammocks from the Bergens. We spread them over the palm leaves, tying their edges firmly to the bottom of the mosquito nets.

James, waiting for the itch to grow tolerable, sat on the edge of the pole-floor of the hut and smoked a cigarette. The Iban seemed to be fast asleep, untroubled. We helped ourselves to another mug of arak each, and I lit my pipe.

"I hate the way you suck that thing," said James. "You look like a schoolmaster, or a rural dean."

"It's comforting," I said, "it empties the head."

"It would empty the room, if we were in one," said James.

"What sort of room would you like to be in?"

"A library. A huge library of my own—in a huge house with a

huge kitchen in a house I have my eye on near Stanton Harcourt; a house with enough rooms to contain all my extended family and lots of friends and still provide inviolable personal space if you needed it."

"And you could have a huge garden with acres of enormous broccoli plants. And brussel sprouts. And enough space to double-dig all day if you wanted to. You could dig a fifty-yard trench and put the finest rotted pig turds in it and grow champion runner-beans and win prizes."

"No, Redmond," said James, stubbing out his cigarette with his shoe on the jungle humus where the fragments shone for a moment, like glow-worm ends. "I would have a garden of land-scaped lawns. And banks. And beds full of rare flowers. It would all be planned."

"You've got to have vegetables."

"I might allow a herb garden. But it would have to be a very particular herb garden, with square plots marked off with stone borders. Or, maybe, with very low, very narrow hedges of box."

We talked about the books we would include in our libraries; we discussed problems of design; we wanted to know whether our holdings should be arranged in bays, or whether that would obstruct an overall view of the gold letters dully gleaming on their leathery spines by the light of the fire. Should the oak shelves ascend to the ceiling, or should we leave space to hang an Old Master or two? We played the reading game of who has read what? And how much can you remember? "And when," asked James, bringing it to a stop, "did you last read Ariosto?" So we gradually forgot the burning itch, and we piled more of Inghai's driftwood on the fire, and the conversation edged slowly backwards into childhood and came to rest amongst rival collections of Dinky toys on the nursery floor. Yes, it transpired, James had also possessed a grey Gordini and a green Cooper-Bristol and a Cunningham C-5R painted in white with a blue double stripe running up the bonnet. He had even (so he said) owned a Trojan van with CHIVERS JELLIES (Always turn out well) emblazoned on its side. But he had left his civilian population woefully unprotected. He entirely lacked armoured cars and personnel carriers, Austin Champ jeeps, Howitzers that fired lighted matches, army one-ton cargo trucks, and Centurion tanks with turrets that swivelled. His farmyard, too, was without air cover; and absurdly vulnerable to attack by Tempest II fighters, Meteors (silver), Hawker Hunters (camouflage green and grey) and Gloster Javelins (with their landing wheels sawn off).

"Psssst!" said Leon suddenly, propped up on his elbow. "The Tuai Rumah says you've talked enough now. He says you talk like a lot of old men on the ruai. He says you talk so long you planning to move the longhouse. Or you going to make war?"

James and I crept into our beds, feeling like two schoolboys caught talking after lights-out.

The day began well. I opened my own eyes to find those of a tree-shrew fixed on me. He was about five feet away, wide awake, perky, sitting on the first branch of a sapling, a yard off the ground, and apparently as fascinated by me as I was by him. His tail hung down, long and brown and bushy; his body was the size of a half-grown squirrel and furry brown, decorated with a black stripe, edged with olive-yellow, which ran from the back of his neck to the base of his tail. He had a long snout, bright black eyes, and small ears set well into his head, ears that were a bit like mine, only prettier. In fact he was probably wondering whether we were related, his tail twitching slightly at the thought. For tree-shrews, once classed with the ordinary shrews (and the mole and the hedgehog) in the order Insectivora, may really be surviving representatives of the animals which evolved into lemurs and monkeys, apes and man. They have relatively large brains, the first digit of their hands or feet can be opposed to the others, their face is reduced in size relative to the cranium, they have a caecum, they give birth to no more than two young, their teats are reduced to four, and they like terong pipit cooked by James Fenton.

The glossy little animal (perhaps a Mountain tree-shrew, *Tupaia montana montana*) suddenly shot its head up, startled, looking beyond me towards the river-bank path. Inghai was struggling up with water for our breakfast rice—and when I looked back at the tree it had disappeared.

Over smoked sebarau and sticky rice we all agreed, with no difficulty at all, to stay exactly where we were for the day. Dana took his gun and a handful of cartridges and went off to hunt pig—and to take his Iban bearings for the jungle trek we would have to make the following day. Leon and Inghai took their harpoons and two Borneo pasties of rice and fish wrapped in palm leaves and set off up the fresh young river Balang to dive for sebarau and turtles. James took out his parang and solemnly cut his black Penguin edition of *Les Misérables* into its constituent books, handing me Fantine and Cosette to keep me sad amongst the boulders.

In the shade cast along the edges of the flood-level river-bed by the forest giants, we read quietly, wedged comfortably into the rounded rocks, our arms and shirts and trousers and feet a sweaty feeding ground of salted moisture for two clouds of iridescent butterflies. A pair of Black eagles soared high above us and seemed to flap their wings, once or twice, every ten minutes or so. A Black-capped kingfisher took up his perch opposite us on a bare patch of a branch overhanging the pool. Perhaps because the water was clearer, perhaps because it foamed whiter on its way through the rocks at the pool margins, perhaps because the sunlight was more dazzling, or maybe just because we were happier—the black head of this particular kingfisher seemed a richer velvet black than that of all the others we had seen; his bill and feet looked newly made, a brilliant carmine-red; his rounded chest and belly and the collar at his neck glowed with a more intense fire of orange and yellow and chestnut; and the feathers on his back and tail caught the sun with a greater medley of changing, dancing purples and blues. He stayed at his perch for hours, making short round flights along the bank and back, hawking for insects like a flycatcher.

In the heat I gradually wearied even of Victor Hugo, and went to fetch the copy of Carol Rubenstein's collection of *Poems of Indigenous Peoples of Sarawak: some of the Songs and Chants*, which we had bought in the Kuching Museum. One or two or three of the under-lying preoccupations of Iban life seemed familiar enough. But even in a society with a custom as delightful and exciting and sensible as ngayap, the secret night visiting of young men to the sleeping places of young girls, life is not always easy. Although it is perfectly acceptable for a girl to have many lovers, and although the Iban believe that conception is impossible in less than three uninterrupted nights of wild lovemaking, she must not have *too* many, and, as Leon told me mournfully, after more than ten different conquests in the same longhouse, even he, Leon, would be in danger of "getting a bad names". Sometimes there are many difficulties to be overcome before one reaches "toward the place that is sometimes forbidden, sometimes not—the mountain of flowers which has wells in it". They range from annoying strategies to prevent the essential preliminary of long, soft talk in the dark:

If you are asleep, dear companion, awaken
and let us make plans together.
If you are awake, dear companion mine, sit up
so we can talk together, side by side.
But no, she does not want to awaken.
She begins to snore, snoring louder and louder,
sounding like the currents of the waterfall
where the rapids drop over the waves;
beginning also to breathe out windily,
sounding like the waves that rush after the tidal bore,
flooding up along the current toward Betong.

Or she may strike a match, light a tallow lamp, and, horrible thought,
demand proof of one's worthiness — once a mere head would do, but
now it will probably be the earning of an outboard motor, a whole
one. Or, worse, carried away, you may get it all wrong from the
start:

Furious, the charming impulsive young lady
feels that the left hand of the lying bachelor
has attached itself to her like a feeding pig tick
come from the swamp at the end of the forest,
feels the hair on his arm,
as if in the grip of a huge fierce bear from a damp place.
Then the charming young woman thrusts him away,
pushing at his neck and also at his waist.

Or, worst of all, she may light a lamp and just feel sick at the sight of
you,

suddenly wriggling as if itchy and crawling with ants
come from the rotted end of a burned unused bamboo container.

I decided that Iban love literature was more teasing than *Clarissa*, and
that such serious studies were altogether too painfully erotic to be
continued in the heat of the day. I took a swim to cool down; I
disturbed the kingfisher, upset the fish, saluted the Black eagles, and
narrowly decided not to enliven the dreamlife of the sleeping James
with the soft noise of a simulated off-stage blowpipe.
Undoing my Bergen, I took out the watertight plastic wallet holding

the last section of our secret government map and spread it on the floor of the hut. It was a remarkable-looking document: a map of the convoluted surface of a giant brain, an impossibly complex finger-print, a mad doodle of hieroglyphs, each one a hill defined by valleys, a chaos of circles and whorls and jiggles, the work of a thousand barometer pens set free across the paper. The walk from base camp to the foothills of Bukit Batu Tiban would be a confusion of twisting hills and ravines and gulleys, a succession of sharp ridges and tiny streams. And it would take us towards the most enticing legends that can be inscribed on any map: NO COVER; AREA UNSURVEYED; RELIEF DATA INCOMPLETE; MAXIMUM TERRAIN ELEVATIONS ARE BELIEVED NOT TO EXCEED 10,700 FEET RISING IN A NORTH AND NORTH WESTERLY DIRECTION; MAP SOURCES UNRELIABLE; LIMIT OF RELIEF AND VEGETATION INFORMATION; RELIABILITY WARNING: OWING TO INADEQUATE SOURCE MATERIAL THERE MAY BE SIGNIFICANT POSITIONAL DISCREPAN-CIES IN DETAIL OVER AREAS OF THIS CHART.

Bukit Batu Tiban (the mountain rock of Tiban), just to the south of the winding stream of the Ulu Baleh, was clearly marked at 5,830 feet, with three ranges of cliffs on its westward slope: but, just to the north of the watercourse, behind a line of south-facing cliffs with a clear way round to the west, there appeared to be an almost equally impressive peak rising to 5,000 feet. And, most alluring of all, it possessed no name. I had momentary fantasies of standing on its summit, Norgay Tenzing-like, breathing comfortably in my oxygen mask, unfurling, in the thin air, a Union Jack, and naming it Bukit Batu Baldy in honour of my companion—though the 5,000 foot contour line rather circumscribed this image. Still, if there *was* a rhinoceros left in Borneo, this ought to be the place to find him. We should have to make a forward camp almost at the source of the Baleh, within a day's journey of the mountain.

In great excitement, I woke James, and broke the new plan to him.

"Forward camp!" said James, rubbing his eyes, crinkling up his forehead with an agonised washing-action of both hands up and down his face. "Day's journey!"

"What's wrong?"

"You just like the sound of the words! That's what's wrong. How do you know what a day's journey is? Were you a boy scout?"

"Certainly not."

"Well, I was, and I didn't like it," said James, pulling a cigarette out of his packet and returning to his book.

In quieter mood, I returned to the hut and began to sort through our equipment. It was obvious that almost everything except the basha kits, the cooking pots, the fish and the rice, ought to be left behind. I put our small collection of books in a plastic bag, covered it in Autan, and slipped the whole sticky bundle inside a capacious dustbin liner, tying the neck tight shut to keep out the ants. Then, however, I visualised a shadowy group of Ukit slipping out of the creepered trees, noiselessly bent on the hunter-gathering of the world's best reading matter, Bertram E. Smythies, *The Birds of Borneo* (third edition). So I transferred the heavy book to my already over-weighted Bergen.

I decided to take my Notebook of Useful Hints too, if only for its words of comfort on the untold slithering millions, the snakes of Borneo. N.S. Haile blithely told me (in the *Sarawak Museum Journal* for December 1958) that "Borneo has the richest snake fauna of Southeast Asia, with some 166 known species belonging to 56 genera in 8 families . . . The greater number of species in Borneo compared with Malaya is surprising, since being connected with continental Asia, Malaya would be expected to have a richer fauna. Many of the species and genera confined to Borneo are rare snakes found in remote mountain areas, where it is supposed that either new species have evolved in comparative isolation, or that species and genera, elsewhere extinct, have been preserved."

Still, 115 of the Borneo snakes have no poison fangs (although, faced with a twelve-foot Keeled rat-snake or one of the vigorous Racers, "common, fairly large, active and bad-tempered" it would be perfectly possible to die of fright without further ado). And of the fifty species of venomous snakes, seventeen were not an immediate problem, being sea snakes, albeit very poisonous, biting freely and, having been seen in hundreds of thousands off the coast of north-west Sarawak, well worth remembering when taking a dip thereabouts.

The rear-fanged snakes, likewise, might be discounted, unless you were being swallowed, which is the only time they inject you with liquid from the grooved teeth in the back of their jaws. Nine species of river snakes from the sub-family *Homalopsinae*, all "said to be bad-tempered", are rear-fanged, as are the venomous members of the *Colubrinae*; and "One of the commonest snakes in Borneo occurs

in this sub-family—the ular daun or ular bunga (*Dryophis prasinus*)."
It is Haile's favourite snake:

> It is . . . in my opinion, one of the most beautiful creatures in the world. It can be any shade of bright-green, olive or greyish-brown, and is easily recognised by its pointed head and extremely slender, whip-like body. It is a tree-snake, feeding on lizards and frogs. Some individuals, I have found, rather resent handling and strike freely and are said to aim at the eye. Also noteworthy are the beautiful Paradise tree snake and Twin-barred tree snake, which are the spectacular flying snakes. They can draw in the belly so that the underside becomes hollow and the snake is shaped like a split bamboo, and then by launching themselves from a branch they can make a controlled glide. The bronze-backs . . . also are reputed to be able to do this.

I made a mental note to remind James to guard the back of his neck against incoming snakes.

So there are really only six species of very dangerous snakes in Borneo: two cobras, two kraits, and two coral snakes. With the enthusiasm of the true scientist absorbed in the fine details of his work, Dr Haile reassured me that any idiot can recognise a cobra when he sees one: they "can be distinguished from other similarly coloured snakes by the third upper labial (third scale back from the mouth on the upper lip) which is large and touches both the eye and the small scale behind the nostril (posterior nasal)". The common cobra grows to a mere six feet; but the King cobra or Hamadryad, the largest venomous snake in the world, has been recorded at eighteen. "Its reputation as an aggressive snake is exaggerated, and it will rarely attack unless cornered or provoked." (I made a second mental note: remember to restrain James from cornering and provoking Hamadryads.)

The Coral snakes are "inoffensive and have small mouths" but the Iban fear them (and they ought to know). The Kraits are gentlemen until you tread on them. The Pit vipers are small, fat, horrible to look upon, and possess an inbuilt, heat-radiation-sensitive body-sniffer stored in an open pit between their nostrils and their eyes with whose aid they edge towards their prey at night. These are the principal nasty surprise in Borneo, tapping their snouts around your ankles, but a shot or two from their fangs leads to nothing worse than near-death. True, they are more of an inconvenience than the cobras, kraits and coral snakes, which are more or less defeated by thick trousers, because they hammer at you with fangs like four-inch masonry nails.

I began to feel drowsy and, listening to a monotonous, loud, repeated call, probably the *took-took-took-took-trrroook* call of the Yellow-crowned barbet which Smythies describes, a sound coming from high in the trees a little further up the bank, I fell asleep.

Leon and Inghai, returning from the Balang, each with a cut sapling in either hand from which hung a line of small sebarau slung by their mouths with a rattan loop, interrupted my siesta. As we prepared an early supper, Dana appeared, too, wading across the river, holding his gun above his head. He was empty-handed and exhausted, but he had marked the start of our route to the Tiban range. He sat quietly eating his sebarau, his legs wet from the river, but his arms still weeping small trickles of blood from his leech bites.

"The Tuai Rumah, he says very many hills, very many streams," announced Leon. "We sleeps now."

TWELVE

I awoke at dawn, to the *dididididi* call of the Grey drongo (probably); the chatterings and mutterings and babblings of unseen Babblers (perhaps); the flutings and whistlings and cat-calls of hidden pittas or bulbuls or cuckoo-shrikes or laughing-thrushes (maybe); and the distant hoot of a gibbon (certainly).

Dana, Leon and Inghai were already up, packing the supplies into Iban carrying baskets.

"Empliau!" I said. "Gibbons!"

The Iban laughed. "No, no my friend," said Leon with a grin, "you tell that Mr Smythies in the book, it's not empliau, it's a bird. The empliau—they called when you asleeps."

"A bird?"

"Ruai. He very smarts. He make a little padi clearing in the jungle and all his wives they come to see his tail."

Checking the Iban against scientific and English names at the back of Smythies, the mystery was soon solved: ruai was *Argusianus* and *Argusianus* was the Great argus pheasant.

After breakfast, I awkwardly manoeuvred my Bergen on to my back. It always seemed intolerably heavy until it was in position, when the brilliantly designed strapping and cushioning and webbing so balanced its frame on the back that it was possible (on rare occasions) to forget that it was there. I then buckled on my SAS belt with its attached compass-bag, parang, and two water bottles in their canvas cases designed to fit against either hip. I filled both from the stream and put two water-purifying pills in each before screwing their tops back on and slotting them into their holders.

James was similarly equipped, looking a little mournful, smoking a cigarette, standing on the shingle and studying the stones at his feet. Dana, Leon and Inghai finished hiding the supplies we were to leave behind and securing the dugout well up a small creek, then hoisted long padi-carrying baskets on to their backs, and joined us. We waded across the Baleh and entered the jungle on the southern bank. Dana took the lead, holding his shotgun; I followed, James came behind me, then Inghai and then Leon, also with a shotgun.

"Why are we armed front and rear?" said James.

"For the wild Ukit men, they attack," said Leon. "This their land. They king of the jungle."

"Heck," said James, wheezing slightly under his Bergen.

"No, my very best friend," said Leon after a pause, "I jokes with you. They go away. They not disturb us. We leave messages. Our Tuai Rumah—he know what to do."

The first hill, which I took to be just the river bank, was so steep that it was easiest to go up it on all fours, when not holding on to the saplings or tree trunks or creepers (and I quickly learnt to inspect each hand-hold for thorns or ants and, in general, snakes). The ridge at the top, however, to my great surprise, was only a pace or two across, and Dana's powerful tattooed-black calf muscles, on which my eyes were sweatily focused, suddenly disappeared from view, over the top and down the other side. I followed as best I could, picked up, it seemed, and hurled down the slope by the great weight of the Bergen, which nudged one in the back like a following bull. I slid over on to my chest and negotiated the steeper twists and turns as if descending a ship's rigging, holding on to the convoluted lattice of roots.

The heat seemed insufferable, a very different heat from the dazzling sunlight of the river-side, an all-enclosing airless clamminess that radiated from the damp leaves, the slippery humus, the great boles of the trees. Three hills in, the sweat towel round my forehead was saturated. My shirt was as wet as if I had worn it for a swim in the river. Dana, just ahead of me, however, appeared unaffected, his own shirt almost dry: and indeed the indigenous peoples of Borneo hardly sweat at all—with a humidity of 98 per cent there is nowhere for sweat to evaporate, no relief by cooling, just an added body-stocking of salt and slime and smell and moisture. I could feel a steady rivulet of sweat running down the centre of my chest, into my belly-button, and on into my pubic hairs, washing the precious crutch powder down my legs.

By hill five, I found it difficult to imagine how I could possibly sustain this pace, carrying this weight. Dana's hugely-muscled little legs were beginning to blur, two mad little pistons pumping up and down through the airless gloom of the forest. There were rare patches of light where a tree had fallen, brief stretches of sunlight on two-hundred-foot-long rotten trunks sprouting with fungi, heavy with moss and lichen, and surrounded by dense, springing vegetation, by thickets of ferns. But otherwise it was a creepered world of apparently endless twilight.

In the warm and scummy bathwater that seemed to slop from skullside to skullside in my head at every step, words of advice from the SAS Major in Hereford suddenly surfaced. It was the kind of comfort which he himself might have needed, I imagined, only after several months rather than several hours of this kind of walk, but it was a comfort, all the same: "In those hills, lads, think of nothing if the going gets tough. Or, if you're young enough [he had seemed dubious], think of sex. Never, ever, think of the mountain that never gets any nearer. Think of nothing, and you'll survive to be a credit to the regiment." I decided, in a *Boys' Own* sort of way, that yes, I very much wanted to be a credit to the regiment. So I thought of sex. But, just as I conjured the first pair of perky breasts and little brown nipples before my eyes and steamed-up glasses, the gully of the hill stream I was crossing went black with oncoming heatstroke. I dimly realised, with heat-hazy annoyance, that I really must be far too old to do it on the march. Instead, a poem, all of my own, burst before me like a volcanic bubble in a mudpool. It went like this:

Oh, fuck it,
it's an Ukit.
We're going to kick the bucket.

This was so brilliant, so obviously a poem of intrinsic interest, that it kept me amused, one word at a time, on the step, for the next three hills.

From a long, long way back we heard a shout. "Stop!" it said. James had made the right decision.

Dana, looking surprised (and a little annoyed, as if he had expected us to run with him all the way to Bukit Batu Tiban without a break) sat down on a tree trunk on the next ridge. I shed my Bergen, sat on it, indulged in some desperate heavy breathing without once thinking of sex, and then opened a water bottle. Its warm, chlorinated contents were perhaps the best drink I have ever taken.

James appeared, closely followed by Inghai and Leon. James looked very hot. He sat on the tree trunk next to Dana, held his head in his hand—and then bounded up with a yell. There was a leech on his left arm. He pulled it off with his right hand, but the leech looped over and sank its mouthparts into his palm. James began to dance, wriggling convulsively. He made a curious yelping sound. The Iban lay down, and laughed. James pulled the leech out of his right palm with his left hand. The brown-black, tough, rubbery, segmented, inch-long Common ground leech, *Haemadipsa zeylanica*, then twisted over and began to take a drink at the base of James's thumb.

"Shit!" said James.

At this point, Leon obviously decided that the two had got to know each other well enough.

"Ah, my best friend," he said to James, as he pulled the leech out, rubbed it on a tree and cut it in half with his parang, "why you come so far to suffer so? Eh?"

James sat down, trembling a bit, and pulled out a cigarette.

"For bully beef," said Dana suddenly, the English of his army days unexpectedly coming back to him. "For Badas bully beef."

"I don't know about that, but I certainly feel I'm being bullied," said James. "There is *absolutely no need* to treat this as an endurance test. From now on, I shall be in second place and we will all be sensible about it."

James, I decided, was an admirable man in every way, having just saved us from death by heart attack, or an all-in melting of the arteries.

"Okay," I said, shrugging my shoulders as if I had actually been about to suggest that we take the next stage at a sprint. "It's all the same to me."

"Jams, my very best friend," said Leon, "you not be angries. Our Tuai Rumah—he always walk fast. He want to tell us he not an old man. He want to tell us he the strongest in the longhouse."

I looked at my legs. And then I looked again. They were undulating with leeches. In fact James's leech suddenly seemed much less of a joke. They were edging up my trousers, looping up towards my knees with alternate placements of their anterior and posterior suckers, seeming, with each rear attachment, to wave their front ends in the air and take a sniff. They were all over my boots, too, and three particularly brave individuals were trying to make their way in via the air-holes. There were more on the way—in fact they were moving towards us across the jungle floor from every angle, their damp brown bodies half-camouflaged against the rotting leaves.

"Oh God," said James, "*they are really pleased to see us.*"

The Iban were also suffering, and we spent the next few minutes pulling leeches off our persons and wiping them on the trees. The bite of *Haemadipsa zeylanica* is painless (although that of the Borneo tiger-leech is pungent), containing an anaesthetic in its saliva as well as an anti-coagulant, but nonetheless it was unpleasant to watch them fill with blood at great speed, distending, becoming globular and wobbly.

Now that I had become accustomed to leech-spotting I discovered that they were rearing up and sniffing at us from the trees, too, from leaves and creepers at face height. We covered ourselves with Autan jelly, socks and trousers, chests, arms and neck. Dana, Leon and Inghai put on their best (and only) pairs of long trousers, and I lent them pairs of socks (they were desperate). I took the opportunity to sidle off behind a bush and fill my boots and y-fronts with handfuls of zinc powder. Sitting down again, I was pleased to see that chemical warfare works: the leeches looped and flowed towards me and then stopped, in mid-sniff, as disgusted by me as I was by them. They waved their heads about, thought a bit, decided that they really were revolted, and reversed.

We set off at a more gentlemanly pace, a slow climb and descent which give us time to drink one bottleful of water at every third gully from the clear tumbling streams, re-fill it, drop in two water-purifying pills, and drink the second bottle at the next pause, repeating the process. Inspecting every tiny rock-pool in which I submerged my flask, I was grateful for Audy and Harrison's warning: there was invariably a Thread leech or two stretching itself towards my hand from the rounded tops of adjacent stones, looking, between each bunching movement, exactly like a pale length of cotton thread. It would have been annoying to have gulped one in, to have it swelling in the throat or setting off for a leisurely peek down the windpipe.

We made our laborious way gradually south-eastwards, keeping the Ulu Baleh to our left. For a time we walked above and beside it, at the top of a great ravine, catching glimpses of its foaming white water, far below, between the hanging fronds of Climbing ferns which seemed to ascend every tree. As the sweat washed the Autan off my neck I replenished it, because there were leeches all the way along the route, in the lianas and on the ground. Indeed, if the number of leeches was any indication whatever of the population density of their warm-blooded victims, then the forest must have been swarming with pigs and deer and squirrels and bears and leopard-cats. But James and I on the move, over-laden, unfit, too old, missing our footing, slithering down slopes, crashing into trees, shish-kebab'd by rattan thorns, panting like an engine shed, must have woken every tarsier, coast to coast.

Dana, now well beyond the route he had marked the previous day, began to notch prominent trees we passed and, when it seemed possible to take either of two alleys up a hill or down a valley he would block the one we were not to use with a bent sapling. When we stopped for a brief (and almost speechless) lunch of fish and rice Dana cut a yard-length of sapling and carefully peeled back strips of bark from its centre. He then hacked down a branch, trimmed it altogether clean of bark, spliced its top, set it in the ground, and placed his rod of curlicues on top.

"What's that for?" said James.

"It tells the Ukit man" said Leon, "that we here in peace, five of us, and that we leave soon."

"In that case," said James, with only half a smile, "perhaps you could make a few more? Strew them about the place a bit?"

"We be all right," said Leon with a grin. "The Ukit man—he only want your head. He never seen a head like yours."

On the march again, caressed by ferns, restrained by lianas, pulling ourselves up banks by the bark of trees, each one of which seemed to have a differently shaped and patterned trunk attended by different lichen and fungi, making our way between trees that were pole-like or thickened at the base or equipped with flying buttress, out-jutting walls of wood, it was easy to believe in the astonishing number of tree species in the jungle. But in the permanent and monotonous midday dusk it was less easy to believe that the South-east Asian rain-forest is floristically the richest in the world. There were epiphytic orchids to be seen here and there in the clefts of smaller trees near the river-cliffs, but little sign of the jungle's 25,000 species of flowering plants (Europe has fewer than 6,000). They live in the canopy, by the banks of rivers, in secondary jungle or in clearings, but now and then we did see a very odd idea in flowers: blossom growing straight from the trunks of trees, sometimes no more than three or four feet from the ground. These flowers, often pollinated by bats, produce a seed complete with a large supply of starting-food to give it a chance in the impoverished soil—an enormous, hard, wrinkled nut that would barely fit in my pocket.

Dana stopped every five hundred yards or so to shred the fronds of overhanging ferns into clusters of thin spirals—but whether to mark our passage or to reassure the Ukit I was too exhausted to enquire. After about a thousand hours (or so it seemed) we climbed slowly down to our left, down to the banks of the Ulu Baleh, which had now shrunk to the size of an English river, waded across it, and collapsed on the northern bank. Dana had decided to make camp.

We all went for a swim—or rather the Iban did, swimming under-water to the far bank and back, whilst James and I sat wedged in the rocks in the shallows, letting the current take some of the terrible heat out of our bodies. Then Inghai unpacked his cooking equipment and began to build a fish-smoking hut whilst Dana and Leon helped us put up our bashas. There was not enough flat space anywhere on the steeply-rising bank to build a communal pole-bed hut, so the Iban made do with a rough shelter.

Sitting round Inghai's fire on the shingle, eating our fish and rice, Leon seemed agitated.

"Redmon," he said, "the Tuai Rumah—he want to know if we climb to the tops of the mountain?"

"I certainly hope so. We'll take it slowly."

"No, Redmon. We Christians like you. We Methodists from Kapit. But we not want to disturb the spirits. Very bad lucks for us to go to the very tops. We go most of the way. You go to the tops."

I remembered Hose's problems one hundred years ago: "The more remote and inaccessible the region, the more are the Toh [minor spirits] of it feared; rugged hill tops and especially mountain tops are the abodes of especially dangerous Toh, and it was only with difficulty that parties of men could be induced to accompany us to the summits of any of the mountains." So said my notebook, and with it I had extracted a map.

This map of the soul's journey was drawn for Hose, with pieces of stick and lengths of rattan on the longhouse floor, by a chief of the Madang (a sub-tribe of the Kenyah). With a few minor variations, Hose found its topography to be common to all the inland peoples. The soul of the dead man wanders through the jungle until he comes to the top of a mountain ridge. From here (much as I hoped we would do from the summit of the unnamed mountain in the Tiban range) he looks down into the basin of a great river. There are five different districts within it, five areas of the dead. Those who die by disease or ageing go to Apo Laggan where they live as they did in life. Those who are killed in battle or by an accident go to the basin of a tributary river, Long Julan, to live by the Lake of Blood, Bawang Daha, where they become rich without having to do any work at all and have their pick of all the women who die in childbirth (a great number). There is a special watery home beneath the rivers for those who are drowned, and they inherit all the valuables lost when boats sink or floods overrun a longhouse. The souls of still-born children, fearless because they have not known pain, live in Tenyu Lalu; and suicides (cases do occur, though rarely, the usual method being to drive a parang into the throat) go to Tan Tekkan, where they live miserably and eat only roots, berries and sago.

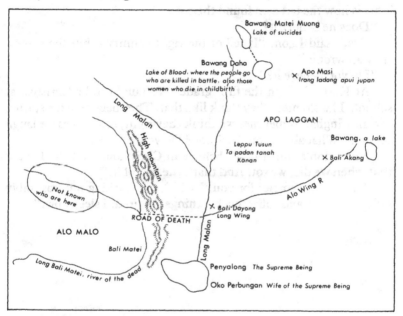

Standing on the mountain top, the soul feels a little odd and begins to suspect that he has come along without his body. Joined there by his parang soul and tobacco-box soul, say, by his dart-holder soul and his blowpipe soul, by the ghosts of the objects hung about his tomb, he sits and laments (if he is a warrior) or howls (if he is anyone else). He then descends to cross the river of the dead. This is a tricky business because the bridge consists of a single tree trunk laid from bank to bank (no problem in itself for an agile Kayan or Kenyah or Iban or Punan) which is being tipped and rolled from side to side by a guardian, Maligang (no bother only if you are an Ukit). If, in life, the soul has taken a head or even been a member of a fruitful headhunting raid, a distinction which will be marked upon the ghost as clearly as on his former body by the tattoos on his hands, then he crosses without mishap. If not, however, the surplus soul falls into the river and is consumed either by maggots or by a large fish, Patan. In some versions the soul approaches the great dividing ridge, as we had done, by boat.

I opened my notebook at the map and showed it to Dana and Leon and Inghai. Dana scrutinised it and a discussion in Iban took place.

"The Tuai Rumah," said Leon, "he says this is an old man's map. This is how the old men found their way."

"Does he believe it?"

"Yes," said Leon. "It tell of the right country—but the names, they all wrong."

"Do you believe it?"

"At Kapit, I reach the fifth grade. We taught to be Christian at school. The old men, they think like that. They believe in the spirits. Me and Inghai, sometimes we think they right, sometimes we laugh at them. What about you, Redmon? Do you believe it?"

"No, I don't. But I don't believe in Christianity, either. I think that when we die, we rot. And that's the end of it."

"Then I very sorries for you," said Leon, looking immeasurably sad, getting up and collecting his things. "I tired. I sleep now."

THIRTEEN

"How were your dream last night?" asked Leon over breakfast.

"Wonderful, very happy," I lied, having slept too well to remember anything.

"And you Jams?"

"I dreamt I shot a gigantic, but *gigantic* wild boar, the father of all fat pigs," said James half-convincingly, "and I scoffed the lot."

"My best friend," said Leon, brightening, "one day we make you a foods you never forget and then you be happy."

"I dream of girls," announced Inghai, stuffing sticky rice into his mouth with his palm and wiping his nose with his forefinger, all in one go.

But Dana sat apart.

"The Tuai Rumah dream very bad dream about the spirits of the mountain," said Leon. "And I, too, unhappy. I not sleeps."

Leon helped himself to a handful of multivitamins from the communal bag.

"We not climb today. Today we rest. And Jams—today he read his big book and eat lots of rices. Makai Jams!"

James looked despondently at the pile of rice in his mess-tin, at the split midriff of a sebarau, at its bones sticking out like an old fence.

We recovered slowly, all morning. Dana cut and peeled rattan and lashed about twenty three-foot sticks into a rectangular cage for smoking fish. Even Leon and Inghai merely pottered about, sharpening their iron harpoon tips on a boulder and mending three big rips in Dana's net.

James slept in the shade of a tree-fern by the river-bank; and I dozed, and amused myself in the Beccari section of my notebook. One of the greatest botanical explorers of the nineteenth century, the

Italian Odoardo Beccari travelled in Sarawak for two years (1865–67) and would not have been in the least impressed by our discovery of flowering trunks, having "noted at least fifty kinds of trees and shrubs in Borneo which show this peculiarity in a marked degree". He was pro-Lamarck and anti-Darwin and possessed one or two crazy ideas on the subject which were all his own. He believed in the inheritance of acquired characteristics—but only during a past era, in a "plasmative epoch" when animals and plants were more malleable. All change, all evolution of one form into others, had now stopped, but in the creative period almost anything might have happened: "Had Man been associated with the dog during the plasmative epoch, I believe that to the expression of our face and to the sound of our voice there would have been aroused in the dog, owing to the attention with which he listens to us and observes us, analogous movements in its vocal organs, which, instead of expressing themselves by inarticulate sounds, would have enabled it to talk and to learn a language."

Innocent of Freud's imaginings, Beccari knew that he liked to go flying, very much, when he was asleep and dreaming. Perhaps this was a relic, a mark of a lost desire from the age of change, an explanation of the "flying lizards . . . flying squirrels, flying foxes, flying frogs, and, could we believe the Malays, flying snakes" of Borneo? Maybe, with all those trees about, and the general impossiblity of running up and down all those hills without banging their noses on a piece of ironwood or getting slung up by the ankle on a bit of rattan, they just wanted to fly so very badly they finally managed it?

In this epoch of "plasmation", considering the very great number of animals that can fly, and how varied they are, it is plausible to suppose that in the higher organisms the desire to press upwards and skywards, whethere to escape danger, seek food, or to enjoy the heat and light, must have been general. This desire, which manifests itself often in man in dreams, and which in dreams he often realises, is not easy to explain, or to connect with physiological phenomena depending on innervation or circulation; but it is conceivable, during the epoch in which the entire organism of every living being was more easily adaptable to external conditions, and could be modified in form according to the stimuli felt, that certain organs, in animals influenced by desire or necessity to leave the ground, may have been so far modified as to become adapted to aerial locomotion, as a consequence of phenomena analogous in their nature to those which come into play with us when we dream that we are flying.

Prone on the shaded river-beach, I was about to fall asleep and dream that I was flying myself when I happened to look up at the next tree along—some kind of chestnut covered in a climbing fern. Perched on the end of a branch, in clear view and some nine feet up, was a bird about the size of a robin. It was behaving like our Spotted flycatcher, making short dashes into a cloud of mosquitoes gathered under the fern fronds, and then returning to its perch. But its back was bright blue and its throat and stomach chestnut, shading into white. As one might expect, Borneo has many species of flycatcher, and, according to the plate in Smythies, the shiny little bird could have been a Malaysian blue flycatcher or a Mangrove blue, or a Large-billed blue, or a Hill blue, or even, most exotic of all, a bird confined to Borneo, the Bornean blue flycatcher. With mounting excitement, I eliminated the possible contenders: the Malaysian blue (Malaya, Sumatra, Borneo) was a bird of lowland forest (and we were camped at 3,000 feet); the Mangrove blue (throughout the Sunda region) was a bird of the coast; the Large-billed (Sumatra, Borneo) was a lowland resident; the Hill blue (widespread in SE Asia) was only sparingly distributed in the Borneo foothills; whereas the Bornean blue was a "submontane resident throughout Borneo; most specimens have been taken at 2,000–5,000 feet".

My turning the white pages from flycatcher descriptions to the flycatcher key to the flycatcher plates frightened the actual flycatcher away. Still, we had seen a bird that was to be seen in Borneo and nowhere else—even if there was no mystery about it and its family relationship was so obvious that is was almost impossible to tell it apart from its cousins. Like the majority of entries in Smythies (and how different from the loving deatail of every spot and stipple and line and blotch, every platform of twigs and moss-lined cup and hanging dome of our own birds, documented by generations of natural-theological clergyman-naturalists, aunts, and schoolboys) the line devoted to NEST AND EGGS read simply "Not described".

The sighting of the Bornean blue flycatcher would have to make up, by one part in a thousand, for our failure to hear so much as a single nasal squawk from the Bald-headed woodshrike, the oddest bird endemic to Borneo which Wallace was the first to discover in Sarawak and which Beccari collected on September 12, 1866:

> I came across a small flock, some five or six specimens, of a beautiful bird which I had not previously seen. Having shot one of them, the others showed no fright, and I was thus able to secure four specimens one after the other. I was not long in recognising them to be *Pityriasis gymnocephala*, one of the few birds restricted to Borneo and characteristic of its avifauna, and for this reason, long sought for by me . . . This bird is about the size of a thrush, with a large stout bill. With the exception of a wide collar of brilliant scarlet, the plumage is entirely of a glossy black. The crown of the head is bright yolk-yellow, denuded of feathers and covered with small and thickly set conical fleshy papillae, whilst the space round the eyes is also bare, with the skin coloured bright red.

For almost a hundred and fifty years after Temminck's official description, no one was sure how to classify it—was it related to the Helmet shrikes of Africa, the Vanga shrikes of Madagascar, or to the *Cracticidae*, the Butcherbirds and Bellmagpies of Australia and New Guinea? The Butcherbirds were not the obvious favourites they might appear to be—because of an invisible dividing line, a biological shadow line, the boundary which Wallace discovered to run north-south between the islands of the Archipelago, dividing Borneo from New Guinea. The Wallace line passes between Bali and Lombok, two small volcanic islands which are climatically identical and only fifteen miles apart, but whose flora and fauna—even the birds—are startlingly different: as Wallace originally reported, in Bali "we have barbets, fruit-thrushes and woodpeckers; on passing over to Lombok these are seen no more, but we have abundance of cockatoos, honey-suckers, and brush-turkeys, which are equally unknown in Bali, or any island further west . . . so that we may pass in two hours from one great division of the earth to another, differing as essentially in their animal life as Europe does from America." And if we sail across this unseen marker in evolutionary time (which in fact corresponds to an undersea meeting place, a subterranean join where the Australasian tectonic plate drifted into the Indo-Asian landmass), if we travel from "Borneo to Celebes or the Moluccas, the difference is still more striking. In the first, the forests abound in monkeys of many kinds, wild cats, deer, civets, and otters, and numerous varieties of squirrels are constantly met with. In the latter none of these occur; but the prehensile-tailed Cuscus is almost the only terrestrial mammal seen, except wild pigs, which are found in all the islands, and deer (which have probably been recently introduced) in Celebes and the Moluccas." And yet, somehow or other, as Ernst Mayr had informed me, *Pityriasis gymnocephala* had crossed the Wallace line. DNA hybridisation analysis had shown it to have ancestors in common with the Australian butcherbirds. One pleasurable little mystery had been replaced with another.

A shout from Dana brought the river back into sharp focus. "Undan! Undan!"

He was pointing to the small space of sky between the great trees upriver, and I was just in time to see two hornbills, with white necks, black bodies and white tails, disappear into the forest to our left. Undan is Iban for the Wreathed hornbill, *Rhyticeros undulatus undulatus*, so I took Dana's word for it.

Inghai filled our mess-tins with hunks of smoked fish and we had a leisurely lunch, casting our scraps to the butterflies. The Iban made plans for a small expedition to the upriver pools with Dana's mended net. James and I decided on a large-scale, all-afternoon siesta, on the tree- and fern-shaded pebbles, surrounded by flycatchers, kingfishers, and hornbills.

I tried to sleep, but the thought of the next day was altogether too pressing: we might, after all (and it would be here if anywhere) discover the last retreat of the Borneo rhino—we might, like Hose in the 1880s be

agreeably surprised to find a sort of ready-made path cleared, as far as one could guess, for our special benefit; on either side of the track the bushes were sprinkled with mud. On making enquiries I was told that a rhinoceros or some other large creature had passed that way. The Borneo rhinoceros is a smallish species and quite the most grotesque of his kind; he has two horns and his hair is tough and bristly, almost like fine wire. He frequents the foot-hills below the mountains, and comes down in the heat of the day to take his ease in what are called "salt-licks", muddy baths formed by springs of saltish water. The clearing and the mud on the bushes were, I was told, caused by the creature's trampling movements to his lair higher up the hills.

We might even, I thought (pushing it a bit, dozing in the heat) see an orang-utan or two (although they are now more or less confined to Sabah, in the extreme north of Borneo). In 1855 Wallace went to Simunjon, a mere forty miles east of Kuching, "to see the Orang-utan (or great man-like ape of Borneo) in his native haunts, to study his habits, and obtain good specimens of the different varieties and species of both sexes [unlike Darwin, he erroneously believed that there was more than one species], and of the adult and young animals. In all these objects I succeeded beyond my expectations." (He shot seventeen.) Shelford, on leaving England for Sarawak in 1897, was asked by "a distinguished anthropologist of my acquaintance . . . to investigate the habits of the Maias [the Dyak name]. 'I want to know how many wives he keeps,' said my friend, 'and how he treats them.'" Shelford was unable to supply the intimate details (they were not revealed until Mackinnon's work in the early 1970s — the orang keeps no wives, is entirely solitary, and only says a brief hello when mating); but he did get an inkling of the very sensible sleeping habits:

> When the Maias goes to rest, it lies flat on its back on its nest and holds like grim death with hands and feet to the branches in the fork of which the nest lies; and so it passes the night, half supported by the frail platform, half suspended by the hands and feet, whose grip is secure even in the deepest slumber. A young Maias that I kept as a pet for many months always slept in an empty room in my house: the only article of furniture in this room was an iron bedstead, and on to the steel laths of this the ape would solemnly climb every evening at about 6.30; he invariably sprawled on the flat of his back, pulled over his head and chest a piece of sacking with which he was provided, and with hands and feet got a good grip on the posts or frame of the bed. In a few minutes he would be asleep, and his snoring was so loud that it could be heard nearly all over the house.

Although not as extreme in their views as James Burnett, Lord Monboddo (1714–99) the author of *On the Origin and Progress of Language* (1773–92), who maintained that the orang-utan was a variety of *Homo sapiens* with a merely accidental speech impediment, and who took his own pet ape out to supper parties dressed in a dinner-jacket to prove his point, late nineteenth-century men of science took Borneo very seriously as a possible birthplace of mankind. Beccari (who himself collected about thirty orangs) tells us that since *The Origin of Species* appeared, "both geologists and anthropologists have always considered it possible that at some past epoch Borneo was the habitat of an anthropomorph more nearly allied to Man than to the living orang-utan. This idea was mentioned to me by Sir Charles Lyell, when I was in London in 1865, preparing for my expedition to Borneo. The great geologist then urged me to explore the caves in that island, being of opinion that important materials and remains of very great value for the past history of Man might be found in them."

And indeed there was, temporarily, good reason to suspect that man might have had his origins in the Malay Archipelago. In *The Descent of Man* (1871) Darwin had favoured Africa (and we now agree with him again) but for a few decades it seemed that although Africa might well have provided the environment which nursed the early evolution of the apes and the pre-human ancestors the "missing link" itself had been found in the East.

Ernst Haeckel (1834–1919), the best known, most aggressive and least scrupulous of Darwin's champions on the continent, lacking Darwin and Huxley's inhibitions, had already named the missing pre-Ice Age creature he needed to complete his evolutionary tree of man's descent: *Pithecanthropus alalus*, the "speechless ape-man". And when Eugène Dubois, a young Dutchman fired by Haeckel's convictions, who had obtained a post as a military surgeon in the Dutch East Indies expressly to look for remains of this speechless ape-man, in 1894, did indeed announce his discovery of an ape-like skull-cap and a much fossilised human-like thigh-bone in his excavations on the bank of the Solo river in Java, Haeckel sent his congratulations by telegraph: "From the inventor of *Pithecanthropus* to his happy discoverer!" Dubois displayed his finds in Berlin in 1895, in Leiden, Paris and London. Java man became firmly established, within the short time-scale of a Lamarckian, late-Darwinian mechanism of evolution by the inheritance of acquired characteristics, as a simple and direct link between modern man and the apes. This was before the re-discovery of Mendel's work and of particulate genetics; the realisation of the immense age of a radioactive sun; and the re-instatement of the theory of natural selection as expanded in the first edition of *The Origin of Species*.

Joseph Conrad had imagined central Borneo to be the heart of twilight, the home of the "old mankind"; and a sight of the Ukit, I reflected, might be as close as we could ever hope to come to those imagined ancestors whom nineteenth-century anthropologists thought had once peopled Europe, primitive men whose beliefs and practices Lubbock and Tylor and Frazer thought they detected beneath our own. But then even the admirable, liberal-minded John Lubbock (he invented the Bank Holiday) could retell this kind of story:

> Speaking of the wild men in the interior of Borneo, Mr. Dalton says that they are found living "absolutely in a state of nature, who neither cultivate the ground nor live in huts; who neither eat rice nor salt, and who do not associate with each other, but rove about some woods, like wild beasts; the sexes meet in the jungle, or the man carries away a woman from some campong. When the children are old enought to shift for themselves, they usually separate, neither one afterwards thinking of the other. At night they sleep under some large tree, the branches of which hang low; on these they fasten the children in a kind of swing; around the tree they make a fire to keep off the wild beasts and snakes. They cover themselves with a piece of bark, and in this also they wrap their children; it is soft and warm, but will not keep out the rain. The poor creatures are looked on and treated by the other Dyaks as wild beasts."

Leon (1983) and Haddon (1888) obviously believed that as you travelled into the heart of Borneo you journeyed backwards and downwards in time, past a series of racial strata that became progressively more primitive. And C.D. Darlington in *The Evolution of Man and Society* (1969) half-agreed with them:

> South-East Asia was largely occupied as recently as ten thousand years ago by dark peoples conveniently known as Australoid. But ever since that paleolithic time the superior technical skill of the Mongolian peoples in the north has enabled them to expand and to invade the accessible valleys of Burma, Thailand, Viet Nam and finally Malaya and all the islands. They have left the Australoid peoples in possession of only the hills, the forests and the swamps, with their greatest stronghold in still largely unknown New Guinea. It may well be this pressure from the north which pushed the Australoid peoples into colonising, first

Australia and then overseas Melanesia. This great movement created the paleolithic basis of the modern peoples of South-East Asia. But superimposed on it during the first millennium B.C. came the forerunners of the neolithic expansion. Moving along the coasts from the Ganges delta, they brought with them the cultivation of rice and the making of pottery and later, towards the end of the millennium, the forging and use of bronze.

Borneo, he believed, was one of the best places on earth in which to voyage from the present, backwards and downwards some thirty to forty thousand years, into the remote past of the Early Stone Age, the Palaeolithic.

The pure Australoid peoples surviving on adjoining islands had disappeared without trace. Farthest inland were the brown nomadic hunters and collectors, the Punan and the Ukit. They had the paleolithic virtues and vices of keen eyesight, alert observation, and incapacity for what neolithic man calls work. Next came the Land Dyaks, neolithic people with primitive agriculture and with headmen having no class character and little power. These people had occupied all the cultivable land during the first millennium A.D. After them had come the warlike agriculturists, the Kayans, forging their own iron weapons and tools and having a class structure with strong chiefs. Next in turn were the Sea Dyaks, originally pirates, aggressive neighbours with shifting agriculture. They were led by Malays, but non-Muslims, for the Dyaks are pig-eating people. Last of all were the three groups of civilized invaders: the Muslim Malays, a highly stratified community led by rajahs; the Chinese immigrants who had made themselves responsible for trade, finance and mining; and in the nineteenth century, the most diverse of all, the Europeans.

Still, one look at Dana and Leon and Inghai was enough to convince any sensible man that in the great nineteenth-century debate about the evolution of the brain it was Wallace who was right, Darwin who was wrong.

Darwin imagined the races of man to be strung out along the evolutionary time-scale in a fine gradation of varying brainpower from civilised man to the "savage". Wallace, however, unlike Darwin on the *Beagle* or Huxley on the *Rattlesnake*, had had to rely on these "savages". Helped at every turn by Leon's ancestors and related peoples in his eight years of travel, often by native *prau*, from one island to another in the Malay Archipelago, he had come to conclude that "The more I see of uncivilised people, the better I think of human nature, and the essential differences between civilised and savage men disappear." He developed his concept of Latent Development—all the races of *Homo sapiens* had evolved a much bigger brain than they actually needed, at the same time. They just used different parts of its capacity in different ways.

All the same, I thought, as I lay in my basha that night and listened to the cicadas, I would be most grateful for a formal introduction to the Ukit.

· FOURTEEN ·

The calls of the gibbons woke me. In the morning mist I unslung my walking clothes from their noose of parachute cord and shook off the ants. I carefully turned out the pockets of my trousers, as always half expecting to find, in the left, one of Wallace's "huge scorpions of a greenish colour and eight or ten inches long", and, in the right, one of his "centipedes of immense size and deadly venom", which "will even ensconce themselves under pillows and in beds, rendering a thorough examination necessary before retiring to rest". In my pockets I found nothing but Elephant ants, but in one of my boots, which hung upside down from two cut saplings thrust in the jungle floor beside the basha, I discovered a black beetle, perhaps some kind of longhorn, about an inch and a half long, armoured with chitinous knobs and ridges and equipped with startlingly long antennae. I tipped him on to the ground and he scuttled away under the leaves.

The Iban were up but James was still asleep. I shook the side of his basha.

"This is the big one," I announced, "this is the day we conquer Everest."

James stirred. There was a heart-rending groan.

"Oh no it isn't," he said, unexpectedly. He clambered half out of the mosquito net, sat on the side of the pole hammock, and held his head. "This is the day *you* conquer Everest. You see, Redmond, I don't have to prove my manhood. In fact, this is the day on which I enjoy my own personal space, miles, but *miles*, from anywhere. I shall potter about; I shall see something *marvellous*; I shall read Swift and Hugo and Vaughan."

"Vaughan?"

"All right, so you think he's a baroque shit? As a special concession to you, as a mark of the profound respect in which I hold your opinions, I shall not read Vaughan. Okay? Can I go now?"

"You must do exactly what you want to do. And if you get a blowpipe-dart in the bum, give us a shout."

After breakfast, we left James, looking very happy, sitting on a rock.

Inghai carried a small padi-basket on his back with a day's supply of cooked fish and rice; Dana and Leon took their shotguns; and I strapped on nothing but my belt kit of compass, parang, and two water bottles. It was delicious to be in the great forest unencumbered, able to move quietly and fast. We climbed steadily north-east, talking, as instructed by Dana, only in whispers.

Termite nests were scattered across the jungle floor, black mounds and pillars about two feet high; other species had slung their fortresses from boughs or plastered them to the sides of tree trunks. Every ten minutes or so, I seemed to hear the swish of hornbill wings, the rush of air through pinions like a flight of swans overhead, the deep cawing call like tumbling ravens. Perhaps it really was an absurdly rich patch of jungle; perhaps I was seeing more because we made so little noise and because my eyes were not drip-fed with sweat; perhaps we were approaching an altitude where the trees do not habitually grow so high, a place where the canopy is not so disappointingly out of reach.

Dana stopped suddenly, holding up his hand.

"Empliau!" hissed Leon, putting a finger to his lips.

We crept forward. And there, no more than forty feet up, in a tree with delicate pinnate leaves which cast a lattice of sunlight on his grey furry back, was a gibbon. He turned his little black face and looked straight at us, for a second or two, with intense interest.

Dana raised his shotgun.

"No! Don't shoot!" I said, pushing his barrel down with my hand. The gibbon, grasping a branch above his head, swung back half an arc, and then launched himself forward at extraordinary speed, trapezing through the air, the small grey body looping after the long flying arms to the next tree, whence he swung, perfectly, into the next, and disappeared. There was a series of slight rhythmic shakings of branches, all around us, as the rest of the troop made their furry half-elliptical flights away amongst the tree tops; and then there was silence.

"Why you stop the Tuai Rumah hunting?" whispered Leon. "Jams—he very hungries."

"But it looked straight at us," I said.

"Very true, my friend," said Leon. "And when you eats the empliau, his hands, they look like children hands."

About ten minutes further up, twisting and turning past tree roots and buttresses and ferns and lianas, we came to a dirty yellow pool beneath an overhang of sandstone. The vegetation all round it was splashed with mud.

"Rhino!" I thought at once.

"Leon, wait," I said, "who uses this?"

"Babi," said Leon, "roast babi." He grinned stupidly, made piggy noises, and rolled his shoulders about as if he was taking a mudbath.

"Pig," said Inghai, pleased with himself. "Fat pig!"

Dana joined in, snorting and grunting, apparently digging up roots with his nose.

"You have Inglang pig?" asked Inghai.

"Yes—but not so big or so hairy."

"Big fat hairy roast babi Inglang pig," said Inghai, making his longest speech to date.

At that moment there was a high-pitched, chattering, rattling noise to our right. Dana motioned us into the mud-splattered bushes. Crouching in the undergrowth I had a momentary vision of the delighted migration of twenty one thousand wild boar ticks bound for a new home in my crutch. I narrowly decided against all-out panic.

"Kijang!" whispered Leon, miming antlers with his fingers against his head.

He eased his shotgun off his shoulder and into position across his knees. Breaking off a leaf, he held it between thumb and forefinger of each hand and sucked it, hard. The kijang, the Borneo muntjac or Barking deer, answered at once; Leon and the deer called to each other, back and forth. Leon, as befitted his character, sounded like a very vigorous kijang indeed, the biggest buck in town: which is perhaps why the deer, seeming to call closer and closer, suddenly stopped, and then, no doubt, retreated. Leon sucked his leaf to tatters, and still there was no answer—but equally there was no bark of alarm (a signal that carries a mile or more, emptying the alerted area).

"Leon," I whispered, "he just can't compete. He's left all the mating to you."

"Ah, my friend," sighed Leon, "perhaps he have a wife in a pink sarong?"

We climbed steadily for an hour or more, turning aside only to investigate an untidy heap of leaves and twigs.

"Babi," said Dana, laying his head on his hands as if to sleep, and snoring.

"The babi make a pile. That for one night. The babi make a bed," said Leon.

It certainly looked easeful and inviting in there. A bristly pig-fug. A swelling tick suckle.

Higher up, we disturbed a large party of langurs, perhaps White-fronted leaf monkeys. There were at least ten individuals, and, compared with the swing and speed and panache of the gibbons, they jumped and scurried away to safety through the branches with awkward crashings, a fleeting chaos of arms and legs and long tails, a glimpse of outstretched browns and greys as they traversed the shafts of sunlight.

"Stones in the stomach," said Leon, looking wistfully at the disappearing langurs. "You take to the Chinese peoples. Very rich. Many dollars."

He must be thinking of bezoar stones, I realised — the oval-shaped deposits found in the gall-bladders of certain monkeys, in the intestines of porcupines (according to Hose) and around broken pieces of blowpipe dart in animals which have been hit and recovered.

"Have you ever found any?"

"No — but the Tuai Rumah, he never find any either. But we keeps looking," said Leon. "When you sicks, you shaking — you take the stone and you eat a bit, a very little bit. You not die."

On a small plateau Dana decided that we should stop for lunch and Inghai handed each of us our Iban pasty of rice and fish in a palm leaf. Dana stood up, pulled an enormous tree-fern frond out straight, and split its central rib back to the main trunk. He released it and the two sections curled rapidly back on themselves, away from each other.

"She light the lamp," said Leon. "She throw you out."

Dana grinned and tried again. This time the fronds curled into each other, the leaflets interlaced.

"She like you a lot," said Leon. "She make you very tireds."

"Is that how you decide?" I asked.

"When no one looking," said Leon with a sheepish smile, "I pull it secret way. She always say yes. I make a cheat."

From the fronds of a climbing fern Dana then made twirls and spirals of serious decoration, messages for the Ukit, and, looking at them, I did briefly wonder if, on our return, we should find James porcupined about the rear with poison darts, busily manufacturing enough bezoar stones to make our fortunes.

About sixty yards further on we came to another small plateau, and stepped into a remarkable clearing: a roundish area, some eighteen feet across, and completely bare. Not a twig, not a leaf, just stamped-flat earth. Dana at once bent his back forward parallel to the ground and arched his arms up behind him. He strutted to and fro, trembling his fingers as if they were the outstretched tips of a fan of feathers, bowing up and down to us. Leon and Inghai laughed and, despite our rule of jungle silence, clapped.

"How-how-how-how-owoo-how-owoo," hooted Dana, stopping only when cut short by his own laughter.

We had found the display ground of the Great argus pheasant.

"The ruai stand here," said Leon, balancing on one leg in the middle of the cleared patch, executing an impromptu Iban dance, "and all the girls in the longhouse come to see him—and he have every one of thems." Leon fell uncharacteristically silent at the thought of so much pleasure.

Continuing our climb we stopped to inspect a long-stay wild boar bed. It was a pig-high, pig-deep recess excavated in an overhang of sandstone and worn smooth, presumably, by pigs turning over in their sleep, dreaming of acorns and fallen figs.

"Father babi," said Inghai, pointing helpfully to the right end of the ledge, "mother babi" (he pointed to the left) "and baby babi" (he pointed to the space in the middle). Inghai was becoming loquacious.

"Stop," said Dana in a voice of command, cupping his left ear. "We listen—CT." I sat down with surprise, closely followed by extreme unease and mild disappointment. I imagined the Ukit, whom I fondly believed to be among the most primitive peoples in the world, sitting in their leaf shelters reading Trotsky.

"Communist Terrorists?" I enquired, weakly.

"He remember Inglang army," said Leon. "He make fool with us. He seen rubber rattan."

Sure enough, Dana was already making transverse slits with his parang in the root of a creeper. Thicker than his thigh, it reared up out of the leaf litter, wound across the jungle floor for about fifteen feet, coiled itself up the trunk of a smooth-barked tree, and disappeared way above us in the tree tops. Dana cut notches, a hand's-breadth apart, all along its length as high as he could reach. At once a thick white gum began to ooze from the wounds and flow slowly down the bark. Dana collected it with both hands, first dressing the join of blade and handle on his parang which had worked loose, and then kneading the viscid mass on to a stick. He gathered a large glutinous ball of the gutta-percha, wrapped it in a palm leaf, and stuffed it into Inghai's padi-basket.

"Badas!" said Dana, setting off up the mountain again at redoubled pace to make up for the pause. I heard the whoosh of the wings of a party of hornbill overhead (if it was not the pumping of blood past my inner ear) but was too preoccupied attempting to keep my ankles out of creepers and my eyes out of fern fronds to look up; I began to sweat in earnest.

Alternately gasping for breath and spitting insects out of my mouth it seemed to me that we climbed for hours, stopping only to bend saplings, to cut bark, to mark our way. But eventually Dana called a halt. With great solemnity, he indicated that we should sit, and composed us in a circle. He rummaged in Inghai's basket, produced a fifth Iban pasty of fish and rice wrapped in a palm leaf, and placed it on the ground in front of us. Something nearby (a troop of monkeys, a flock of birds?) made a chattering, a cackling chorus of alarm from the trees, and then ceased. Leon looked uncomfortable and wiped his lips with his hand.

Dana uncorked his water bottle and tipped a thimble-full on the ground behind him. We followed suit. My cholorinated water fell smack on top of a small, brown, weevil-like beetle which, at the wholly unexpected indignity, shot under a leaf.

Dana then fixed the little pile of rice and fish with a chiefly eye and mumbled in Iban; Leon and Inghai repeated the incantation.

"Inglang spell!" said Inghai, turning to me, "Inglang magics! Very strong. Very good."

"We pray to the spirits of the mountain-top," I said, remembering the Fenton formula from Kapit, "for good success and a safe return."

Dana picked up the pasty and lodged it about five feet from the ground, thrust between a creeper and a tree trunk.

"Now we be okay," said Leon, "now we go all right."

The trees became smaller as we climbed, more heavily hung with mosses and lichens; and the air became noticeably colder, patched with mist.

And then, suddenly, the steep slope levelled: we had reached the top. Dana cut two saplings, splitting the top of one as a support-stick and fraying the bark of the other into a message pole. We then made our way across the flat ground for about two hundred yards, to the other side of the mountain. There was nothing to be seen but a rich tangle of tree and creeper, fern, moss and lichen.

"No worry Redmon," said Leon, drawing his parang, "we at the top. We show you wild ulu country. My good friend, no worry, you see very far, very far. Maybe we show you the sea."

Leon, Inghai and Dana hacked away with their parangs at a half-grown tree. It creaked, swayed at the top; the lianas stretched tight.

"Stand back! Go away!" shouted Leon, "Snaks! Snaks! They in the tree!"

I reversed, fast—so fast, in fact, that I was too far back, when the whole mass of vegetation did begin its crashing fall down the slope, to see if there were any evicted snakes curling through the air in venomous parabalas or not.

But there was no doubt about the view disclosed through the gap: the ground fell away to the east; we looked out across the jungle-covered hills rolling to the horizon. We stood at the heart of Borneo, therefore, on the watershed; all the little streams below us would eventually flow south-eastwards to join the great river Mahakam. We had, unknowingly, crossed into Indonesia, and we must have been standing somewhere on the 6,000 foot ridge to the north-east (and slightly above) Mount Batu Tiban. Despite the toh, we made a lot of noise, repeated the Argus pheasant dance, and exchanged hats. A pair of Black eagles, unconcerned, their beaks and long tails glossy in the sunlight, were beating low over the forested valley immediately below us, wheeling, mewing to each other.

Huge clouds were piling up in the east, and we returned to camp at great speed, stopping only to take more pictures of pig wallows and termite's nests, fungi, and some kind of pale pink orchid.

When, after our nine-hour adventure, we finally reached the shore of the Ulu Baleh, Dana strung us out and signed for us to be silent. He then advanced again, with exaggerated carefulness, placing each foot with considered wariness amongst the leaves.

"Now we take Jams's head," whispered Leon, with an enormous grin.

We crept up on the camp in a line, with Dana and Leon slightly forward on the wings. Poor James was peacefully reading, his back to us, in the shade of a large boulder. He just happened to be opposite my position in the assault. I edged forward across the shingle until I crouched behind the rock and then, with what I imagined to be an Ukit-cum-Clouded leopard assassination howl, I lightly touched his neck. The Iban yodelled a particularly horrible battle cry. I can't say that James's hair stood on end, because the sample is not statistically significant, and he only emitted a smallish scream; but his legs went convulsively stiff and shot up in the air, and he threw his arms wildly over his head. His section of *Les Misérables* landed some yards away. And his countenance, when he rolled, very fast, on to his stomach, conformed, in several crucial respects, to Darwin's description in *The Expression of the Emotions* (1872) under the heading "Fear": his uncovered and protruding eyeballs were fixed on the object of terror (me); the wings of his nostrils were widely dilated; he exhibited a death-like pallor; his breathing was laboured; and there was certainly a gasping and convulsive motion of the lips, a tremor on the hollow cheek and a gulping and catching of the throat.

"Jesus Christ!" said James. And then, very slowly, "I have allowed myself," he said mournfully, "to come to the middle of nowhere, the middle of *nowhere*, with a bunch of maniacs."

Inghai took off his padi-basket. Dana, Leon and Inghai lay down.

Darwin, when compiling his great work on expression, wrote to the Rajah Brooke to enquire if the Dyaks of Borneo shed tears when they laugh heartily; "it must frequently be the case," he decided, "for I hear . . . that it is a common expression with them to say 'we nearly made tears from laughter'". It is. They do. They did.

"Jams!" yelled Leon, "what you think kill you?"

"I'd just been thinking about it," said James, cheering up, loosening his dried lips with a swig from his water bottle. "I thought, *hang on*, they've been away *for hours*. The Ukit have got them. And now— *they'll come for me*. And then they did. One big, overgrown, retarded, underdeveloped, irresponsible Ukit."

"One big fat hairy roast babi Redmon pig," spluttered Inghai.

"Okay," said James, rolling his enormous eyes and making an emphatic gesture with his right hand, "so whose idea was it?"

"The headmaster," I said, pointing at Dana.

"Leon," said Dana.

"Inghai," said Leon.

"Redmon," said Inghai, howling with laughter, jumping to his feet, "he big fat Inglang headhunter."

James, his trousers sagging, his shirt hanging out, made a run at

Inghai, or rather he made his characteristic pattering plantigrade shuffle, his feet set at an angle of forty-five degrees to the line of each leg. Inghai dived into the pool.

"We make peaces," shouted Inghai with a note of desperation, just his head above water. "The Tuai Rumah—he hide arak."

"Jams, my very best friend," said Leon, "it's true—he hide a tin in the rices tin. We drink. We make sorries."

We all trooped up the bank to Dana's sleeping place, Inghai a safe few paces behind, bearing *Les Misérables*, which he had retrieved from the beach.

We knelt down. Dana opened his sacred Chinese biscuit tin. It seemed to contain nothing but rice grains. Dana put a hand in and dug about. Two cartridges and the corner of a packet of Gold Leaf cigarettes hove into view. With uncharacteristic speed, James whipped his hand in and nicked the packet out.

"Shit!" said Dana, or something very like it.

A small Chinese medicine tin appeared. Dana prised off the lid. There was enough rusty, metallic arak for a mouthful each. We passed it round.

"Ngirup Jams!" said Dana.

"Er—how do you feel? How's the heart, James?" I asked, suddenly remembering his palpitations and suffering the onset of remorse.

"Fine, just fine," said James airily, "and no thanks to you whatever, scumbag. In fact you lose all the Brownie points you ever gained. However, I am about to have my revenge—because I *did* see something marvellous."

"Oh yes," I said, beginning to feel jealous. "A leopard came down to drink? A tarsier tweeked you on the ear? You shared a fag with a binturong?"

"Until this moment," said James, thinking about it, "I only had three ciggies left. I don't *think* I would have shared one, even with a whatsit."

"Of course you would—it's a friendly, shaggy bear cat that can hang upside down from a tree like your angwantibo in 'The Wild Ones'."

"The angwantibos in 'The Wild Ones'," said James, "are riding tricycles."

"I don't see why that stops them having a fagette."

"You don't want me to tell you, do you? You're jealous! You think it might *really* have been marvellous. Well, it *was*. I saw the two most beautiful birds in the world, the most beautiful birds I *have ever seen.*"

James's eyes were as big and brown and bright as those of a loris after dark. He was obviously telling the truth.

"They were over there," he said, pointing to a chestnut on the opposite bank, "chasing each other so fast round and round and round the top of the tree that to begin with I couldn't make out if it was one bird or two—and they were the yellow of all yellows, the kind of yellow that every other yellow secretly wishes to be."

I fetched Smythies and turned to Plate XLIII : The Orioles.

"That's it!" said James, triumphantly, "they were Black-naped orioles! Only this one is off-colour; he's had a rotten night; he forgot to take his Alka-seltzer. Mine were the flaming youth of the forest, the *jeunesse d'or*, the jungle glitterati."

We looked up the description. "It is odd that this bird," said Smythies, "so common in Singapore, should be so rare in Borneo; it is known from three skins collected by Croockewit in S Borneo, and a few skins and sight records from SW Sarawak; whether it is a resident or a visitor is unknown."

James looked annoyed.

"Come on," he said. "What's Singapore got to do with it? It's meant to be a book about the birds of *Borneo*. If I saw a Martian in Piccadilly, you wouldn't say 'Forget it James, so what? They're common on Mars,' would you?"

"Well, it could have been worse."

"*Come on.* I really do not see how it could possibly have been worse."

"You might have seen a Great tit."

"Don't be silly."

"No really—it's one of the eight rarest birds in Borneo, along with the Malaysian honeyguide, the Bald-headed woodshrike, the Siberian thrush, the Orange-headed thrush, the Chestnut-capped thrush, the Black-browed babbler and Everett's thrush—and here they all sit on Plate XLV."

We looked up Great tit. "The mystery bird of Borneo," said Smythies. "Two or three specimens were collected in the 1880s at Tegora and the Bengo range of hills south of Bau. It was not heard of again until December 10, 1956 when Allen observed a pair in the mangroves at Pending, near Kuching, and a specimen was obtained there two days later by a Sarawak Museum collector. Several were seen again in this area (at Tanah Puteh army camp) in April 1965, and others on May 17 near Buntal and Santubong, confirming the mangrove habitat of this species (MF). It has also been recorded in riverside jungle and mangrove at Binsulok and Kuala Penyu January–February 1962 (DMB)."

"Now, you have to admit," I said, "that you would feel foolish attempting to excite your Aunt Eileen about a Great tit? Wouldn't you?"

"I have just decided," announced James, "that the hunt for ornithological rarities is essentially frivolous."

That evening, sitting by the fire after a supper of smoked fish and rice, I was idly looking at one of our smaller-scale maps of Borneo, taking a boat journey by the light of my torch along the Rajang (way to the north-west of our present position) to Belaga, where the Rajang divides into the Batang Belaga and the Batang Balui. I followed the Balui to Long Murum, and twisted down, south-westwards along its now-straightening course, towards the Batu Laga Plateau, to Rumah Daro, and then—the torch and I both suffered a severe attack of paroxysmal arythmia—I arrived at a place which was unmistakably entitled Rumah Ukit.

"Leon! James! I've found an Ukit longhouse!"

"Not round here?" said James, looking startled, peering out into the equatorial night.

"No, no, it's miles to the north-west, it's on about 1°45', but we can get there easily—up the Rajang and down the Balui."

"The government—they make it for the Ukit," said Leon.

"What makes you think they want to see you?" said James.

"The government—they want to watch the Ukit man," said Leon.

"Quite right too," said James.

"Well, they may not want to see me," I said "but they'll certainly want to see a bald poet. Everybody always does."

"Look here Redmond," said James, "all those people are poets. There is absolutely nothing special about it. I feel, very strongly, that we should leave the Ukit to do their thing, to make their mince pies, *entirely undisturbed by us*."

"Inglang poet," said Inghai, beaming.

"Exactly," I said, "we're going."

"Heck," said James, rubbing his face with the palms of both hands.

"Jams, my very best friend," said Leon, taking him by the arm, "they not the proper Ukit man. The Ukit he live in the jungle and he travel very far. He go where he want. He like to hunt babi every day of his life. But the government not know where he is—so the government say 'we give you a longhouse and you grow padi and you stay still so we can count you.' But the Ukit man stay in the jungle. He like it very much. Only a few Ukit in Rumah Ukit."

"Okay," said James, "so have you been there? Do you drop in for tea at the weekends?"

"No," said Leon with an enormous grin, "I not even been to Belaga."

"Okey-scrokes," said James, "if the Ukit are such good eggs, why don't you come with us?"

Leon went darker brown with pleasure. He held excited converse in Iban with Dana and Inghai.

"We Iban need the Tuai Rumah in Kapit for the padi," announced Leon, "and Ingy-Pingy go to work in a timber camp, but I come. I come Jams; I look after you and Redmon."

"Done," said James, shaking Leon's hand.

Drops of rain began to patter down. The cicadas stopped their stridulation.

"I'll ask Thomas to come," said Leon.

"Who he?" said James.

"Thomas, he's my friend," said Leon, "he's Lahannan, the Kayan peoples. His longhouse is near the Ukit. He says the Ukit girls—they very beautifuls."

The rain became persistent, heavy, and then excessive. We went to bed.

FIFTEEN

It was still raining in the morning. Looking out past my feet through the triangular gap between hammock and awning at the foot of the basha I could see huge drops splashing on the wet boulders, spattering into the river, puckering its surface; but underneath the trees the rain, fragmented into particles by the fine mesh of leaves, branches and creepers, seemed to hang in the air as a heavy mist, oozing down trunks, sweating, soaking everything. Rolling little doughy cakes of super-saturated zinc talc over myself, I climbed into my clammy clothes and rubbed Autan gel through the film of water on to my socks and shirt sleeves and neck.

"Jams! Redmon! Wake up! The river rise in the night!" shouted Leon from the shore.

And indeed half the shore itself had disappeared.

"The Tuai Rumah say we hurries, or we never cross the river," said Leon, coming up the bank, shaking James awake, and helping us to bundle the wet basha equipment into the Bergens.

The Iban carried their own padi-baskets, held in front of them, across the river, and then returned to take our Bergens. I remembered the SAS Major's advice: "Never cross a river with a Bergen on your back. It's the only time it turns nasty. One slip. In you go. And then the Bergens will push your head down, firm and gentle, just beneath the surface."

Reaching the other side, we hoisted on our packs, scrabbled up the wet bank, and then turned and said goodbye to the most beautiful retreat on earth, the home of the gibbon and the Great argus pheasant, the Borneo deer and the wild boar, the hornbills and—rarest of all—James's friends, the Black-naped orioles. In a month or two the vegetation would cover the Iban shelter, the crossed poles of our basha frame, the Ukit message sticks and shredded ferns on the mountainside, and, rightly, not a trace of us would remain.

Even at our new, slow pace, with James walking behind Dana, it was a tough march. The mat of leaves, soaked by the rain, moved against the soil at every step; we slipped and fell down the hillsides; we slithered into the little torrents of white water which had appeared in every gully. There was nothing to break the monotony of effort; no hornbills swish-swished overhead, no monkeys peered down in disbelief, everyone had taken shelter. I found myself repeating a secret, optimistic mantra to myself: "This will all be over one day," went the numbing little chant, round and round in my head.

Halfway through the afternoon James began to fall more frequently and more heavily. He would just look resigned, clutch hold of a creeper, pull himself to his feet and carry on, without a word of complaint. But after a series of particularly hard slides into trees on the sandstone slopes, Leon became much moved.

"Jams, my very best friend," he said, standing beside him, "this damn sillies. You break your leg."

Leon bent down and eased James out of his pack. He then slung off his own padi-basket and bound it to the top of James's Bergen with parachute cord.

"Don't be absurd, Leon," said James.

"Don't you worries Jams," said Leon, "I very strong. You see."

"Why don't you share it with Dana and Inghai?" I said helpfully, not much caring to carry even half an extra pair of y-fronts myself.

"No worries. You see," said Leon, squatting down, pulling the Bergen straps over his shoulders and then raising the huge load into the air as he stood up, awkwardly.

Dana, James and Inghai went on, and soon disappeared in front. Leon and I followed very slowly. I walked behind him, astonished. I had no idea it was possible for one man to carry so much; the unwieldly baggage rose above his head, keeling from side to side as he walked.

Leon stopped, unloaded, cut himself a sapling, trimmed it to a five foot length and then lifted his pack and basket again.

"Now I better balance. You see," said Leon.

He tight-roped his way along the path marked by Dana, grotesquely weaving his pole in and out of the trees and bushes on either side, but staying firmly on his feet.

After an hour or two, Leon stopped.

"Redmon," he said, "we take wrong turn. Now we go backs. I miss the mark."

I sat down in despair. Just a little sleep here, I thought. The hill we had just slithered down rose up behind us, a Himalaya that grew even as I watched it. To have to climb *that* . . .

"Get up," said Leon decisively. "You get up. You have one pack onlies. You get up Redmon. You very fats. You stop—they worries. You worry Jams. The Tuai Rumah—he think we lost."

"You'll be a bloody rumah zoomer yourself one day," I said, getting up in spite of myself.

Eventually we emerged, exhausted, on the shore of the Baleh opposite the base camp. Dana and Inghai collected us in the dugout.

"What kept you Redmond?" enquired James airily when we reached the other side. "I was beginning to get worried. I was about to ring your wife."

The following morning the rain eased, the gibbons hooted, the spine-tailed swifts appeared over the pool in front of us, and Dana decided that we must leave. The river had risen about five feet; the boulder where I had sat reading Smythies had disappeared and its position was now marked only by a dark spin of water.

We stowed the padi-baskets and the Bergens in the dugout and lashed them to the gunwales with rattan. We then tied tarpaulins tight down fore and aft over Dana's tins and Inghai's cooking pots and Leon's huge store of smoked and salted fish.

We pushed the boat out and jumped in, James and I resuming our old positions facing each other in the middle, Leon manning the outboard and Dana and Inghai crouched in the bows, their poles and paddles beside them.

With Dana and Inghai paddling ferociously to keep the dugout from turning sideways to the current, Leon managed to start the engine at the third pull; we swung violently out into the centre of the swollen river and began to move with extraordinary speed. The long, unwieldy canoe hung in the main body of water, its bow lifting, trying to plane; twin arcs of spray hurtled past us.

At each twist of the watercourse it seemed that the boat would spear itself into the overhanging bank; but, as Dana and Inghai gripped hard on their poles and lodged their feet against the opposite gunwale, ready to fend us off, the rebounding water would kick the bow back into the curve of the flood. We hurtled downstream and the boat rolled left and right alternately, as we swung juddering off the fling of the bends. A white churn of surface fire-hosed past the dipping gunwales. James and I pulled our mess-tins out of the strapped Bergens stowed behind our backs and began to bale out in earnest.

"Redmond," said James, his whiskers as shiny as a seal's in the spray, "on the Cresta run, so I hear, the secret of survival is simply a matter of timing. You must jump only when you are *absolutely certain that that is what you really want to do in life*."

We entered the Kenyah lands and the river grew wider and more manageable. Lines of women, weeding in the padi fields, stopped their work, straightened their backs and waved to us. Excited dogs tried to keep pace with the boat, dashing down the shingle banks, yelping. We put in to the landing area and Dana went to inform whoever might be in the chief's room that we were leaving, and to offer to take the dying woman to hospital. We waited in the boat, as protocol demanded; and in about half an hour Dana returned with the chief's son bearing two huge bunches of bananas, a parting gift.

"What about the woman?" said James.

Leon spoke to Dana in Iban.

"The Tuai Rumah—he says she too sick to move," said Leon. "She not want to go. Hospital so very far. How she make monies to buy the petrols to come back to her people? Eh?"

James stood up, rummaged in his Bergen and drew out his bottle of thirty Floxapen. He stepped out of the canoe and presented them to the chief's son. James limped horribly, he acted a gangrenous leg, he indicated the popping of one pill in his open mouth per one traverse of the sun across the sky. Leon translated into Iban, Dana translated into pidgin Kayan; the chief's son appeared to understand. He shook us all by the hand and then pushed the boat out into the current. Leon started the motor, swerving the boat from side to side, throwing Dana and Inghai off balance.

"She in the fields!" yelled Leon, "but I say goodbye! I say goodbye to the moon in the sky!"

It was a violent descent down the Baleh. Through the scrape of mess-tins on the duckboards and the constant thump of incoming water we would hear the shouted commands of Dana; the staccato shrieks of warning from Inghai as rocks reared up ahead and shot past astern; the wild yells with which a feverishly excited Leon greeted the passage of each new rapid. Through the curls of spray we watched the kingfishers fly to cover. Eagles launched themselves from their fishing perches, turning and banking to safety in the jungle. Little green herons, frightened, flapped awkwardly into the bushes by the riverside.

A headlong intemperance of action rose from the whirling river and possessed the Iban. We stopped only to retrieve the hidden drums of petrol, to scoop some rice into our mouths, to replace the bundle of poles which Inghai and Dana splintered, one by one, as they fended the bow off the rocks. To keep his purchase on the current, Leon drove at full throttle, hour upon hour.

"I'm not as green as I'm cabbage-looking," announced James, *à propos* of nothing in particular, as we baled our nineteenth cubic ton of water from the bottom of the boat (he was actually looking very clean, very washed, very tired) "and this will end in tears."

Late in the evening, however, we cheered up. The first timber camp swung into view on the right-hand bank.

"Stop!" cried James. "Stop you crazy bastards!"

Leon ran the dugout up to the landing-stage. James sprang out of the boat with an agility, a set of unsuspected reflex loops, not used, I would imagine, since early childhood. He set off up the planking like an arthritic gazelle. "Someone, somewhere in this place," said James, "just has to have a ciggy—and maybe, just maybe, a can of beer." He ran up the bank with a touch of real acceleration, water drops catherine-wheeling out of his shirt and trousers.

An earth-mover slewed to a halt. The driver leaned out of his cab and looked at James with amazement.

"Cigarettes! Beer!" yelled James; so instantly proving his status as *Homo sapiens*.

"Guinness Stout!" replied the Iban driver with hearty approval, pointing James to a hut up on the left. "Guinness stout!" he repeated, rumbling his great machine back into life.

Behind James, we all broke into a run towards the hut. The Iban swept past me, hurdling the log-restraining hawsers, weaving between parked bulldozers.

When I reached the shop James was addressing a little old startled Chinaman behind the counter. "Cigarettes! Beer!" he said, gasping for breath.

It seemed a miraculous place, this under-stocked, dingy little cavern. There were brightly-coloured packets on shelves; and tins with pictures on them; and food in corners. And no fish anywhere.

The Chinaman, sizing us up, bent down very slowly and put an empty box ready on the table.

"One for now, if you don't mind," said James, reaching over the Chinaman's head and plucking a packet of Gold Leaf.

The Chinaman picked up his abacus and began playing with it nervously, whizzing the threaded marbles of black wood up and down. James found his lighter, lit up, gave the Iban and the Chinaman a cigarette—and then began to pile Guinness and Gold Leaf and Peach Pieces and Pineapple Rings and Roasted Peanuts and Steak Chunks into the container. I found myself gathering armfuls of Green Giant Sweetcorn. James paid from a roll of Malaysian dollars in his back pocket that must have been growing fungus for several spore-producing cycles. The Chinaman smiled.

We walked slowly back to the boat, past the earthmovers and bulldozers and hoists, past the hewn trunks of forest giants waiting in piles to be rolled into the river and rafted downstream, across the orange-yellow, levelled, bare, dead ground.

Windy with sweetcorn, slopping with peaches and pineapples, gritty with peanuts, full of Eastern Guinness, we travelled until the moon came up, and then, guided perhaps by the rich comforting smell of domestic pig-shit, Leon found the creek which led to the longhouse where his parents-in-law lived. In their bilek, we gave them the rest of the Guinness, tried to recount Leon's heroic exploit in the whirl-pool, and fell asleep where we lay. The next day, after a prolonged stop on the shore while Dana carefully divided the great hoard of fish into three, we entered the river Rajang and arrived in Kapit.

· SIXTEEN ·

We sweated up the concrete steps of the downstream pier carrying our Bergens, crossed the dusty waste ground which the eight-year-old Chinese boys used as a test track to ascertain the breaking point of new bicycles, waved to Ella Fitzgerald (and thin Mr Fitzgerald) in our Chinese breakfast café, and entered the concrete stairway to the Rajang Hotel. Greeted by the friendly, ancient, twisted, hairless, one-toothed, semi-mute Chinese receptionist, we felt we were home.

Our old numbers were taken, and our spare baggage awaited us in two adjacent rooms on the floor above. As we reached the top of the stairs and turned left an open door disclosed a bare room containing a dressing-table and mirror, a cassette player, three beds and three girls.

"Hello," said James in his cheeriest manner, "and how are you?"

The girls screamed and then giggled and then slammed the door.

"Redmond," said James, "they saw you first."

Once safely in my own room I took a luxuriously clean set of clothes out of my kit-bag, laid them out on the bed, emptied my Bergen over the floor, crunched half a dozen evicted ants with my boot, squelched my jungle clothes up into a slimy ball, left them by the door for the unfortunate Chinese laundress, and spent a long time shaving off my beard by the cracked mirror over the tiny basin. I then wrapped myself in the small towel provided and walked nonchalantly down the corridor to the shower box. I slung my towel over the wooden partition and began the laborious, sensual process of filling and re-filling the standard, red plastic, saucepan-shaped ladle full of cold water from the low-pressure tap and emptying each load over my head. Eventually, when the hotel soap had shrunk from plum to peanut-size I reached out for my towel. It was not there. I opened my eyes. It must have fallen to the floor. I dropped to my knees and looked under the partition. It was not there either. *The bastard*, I thought. I must keep calm and think this over. It would not be seemly to panic. I looked about. There was nothing to look about at. A red plastic saucepan-shaped codpiece would have to suffice.

Holding the ladle with one hand, I flung the door open with the other; and I came out of that box like a winner at Newmarket. But it was no good. The door of the girls' room was open. The girls stood outside it, shrieking with laughter. "Inglang!" they howled as I sped past, "Inglang!" I reached my own room—and the door was open. Inside stood the old, wrinkled, impassive Chinese laundress. She looked at me as if all her clients were in the habit of taking their evening run wearing red plastic saucepan-shaped codpieces. She gave my jungle clothes a disgusted push with her foot; and then she held out her hand. "Oh Jesus," I thought, "she wants my saucepan." I indicated that I did not consider her request to be reasonable. She then held up both sets of worn fingers, twice. "It's money she wants," I realised, with relief; and then, "It's twenty dollars she wants!" I was not well placed to argue. Edging over to my kit-bag I one-handedly extracted the notes from my waterproof wallet. Expressionless, she took them, picked up the clothes, and bowed herself out. The girls were still giggling in the corridor and, above their burbling notes, a little like the flight calls of the female cuckoo in an English summer, there came a high-pitched, nasal, long-drawn-out, hysterical cackle. The impassive Chinese laundress was laughing fit to bust.

I dried myself with a pair of y-fronts, dressed in clean clothes, and went downstairs to the café on the corner, to kill the Fenton.

"Hello," said James, spluttering into his Chinese beer, "everything all right? Have a good shower?"

"You bastard!"

"The girls watched me do it," said James. "They thought it was a *tremendous* idea."

Later in the afternoon a newly-smartened Leon arrived at the café with Siba and Edward, to take us to the longhouse for Dana's welcome-back party. I ran up to my room, packed the Polaroid, all our remaining film and flashbars and two bottles of whisky in a kit-bag, and rejoined the others. We had a beer all round, discussed our adventures, and then set off out of town and up the track.

"So why can't you get a doctor to the Kenyah?" said James.

"That's all too simple to answer," said Siba, filling his pipe with Erinmore, the only brand of pipe tobacco to reach Kapit, "we don't have the money—we can only afford to buy a few helicopters and we can only afford to pay a few doctors. As you discovered, James, the Baleh is a difficult river, not really navigable. And besides—those people are technically illegal immigrants. If we wanted to, we could throw them out. It's a problem for my department. But then my department has an easy solution: our laws state that anyone born in Malaysia becomes a Malaysian citizen—so in one generation those people will become our responsibility. And by then we will be able to reach them. We are a new country, you must remember. The Rajahs Brooke educated the Land Dyaks around Kuching, and then the Sea Dyaks, the Iban—or some of them—and now we are building schools and dispensaries for the Kayan and the Kenyah and all the other inland peoples. You'll see when you go—there are schools all the way up the Rajang and the Balui, and one or two dispensaries with barefoot doctors, and a small hospital in Belaga with a helicopter pad which we can reach from here."

Siba gestured at the little airstrip we were passing, complete with control tower, radio mast, two light aircraft and a helicopter.

"The doctors fly out from here to all the longhouses they can reach, one a month. But now the government say times are hard, and it's all too expensive, and they will have to make do with one visit every six weeks."

"All the money goes to West Malaysia, to Kuala Lumpur," said Edward gloomily. "And anyway—take a good look around when you go up the Balui to see the Ukit, because the whole area is going to be flooded. The politicians get rich—one or two men get rich granting licences to the Chinese to tear out our forests and take it all downriver; and now they're going to build a dam and lay a cable to Japan and sell electricity and get even richer. You can say what you like, Siba— very soon there will be none of our land and none of our jungle left. Nothing."

"Of course the dam must be built!" said Siba. "How else will we pay for our people to be educated and have hospitals and live a decent life? I grant you—if we were Brunei and struck oil on the coast, we could leave the jungle alone *and* give every citizen a colour television set. But there's precious little oil. There's water and there's wood."

"I work in a timber camp," said Leon. "I buys my outboard motor. Very hard. Very dangerous. My friend—he fall out of his tractor. He hit a bump on a hill. He fall down and the back wheel go over his head. His head fly open. Like a fruit. All the pips fly out, all the juice."

"So why can't the jungle grow back?" said James. "Why can't you just take the trees you want and leave the rest?"

"Your scientists say it won't grow back for a thousand years," said Edward. "It's not like clearing the jungle for the padi. The bulldozers kill the soil. The rain sweeps it away."

"There'll be a solution," said Siba, "we'll find an answer."

As we turned off the town track and entered the secondary jungle I was startled to see a large crow-like bird approaching us from the right, closely pursued by two bumble bees. The bees flew straight and fast behind, keeping their distance, precisely maintaining their formation.

"Quick James," I said, "look at that—it's being driven off by bees, or are they hornets?"

The bird flew right over us.

"They're feathers, you clunk," said James, "they're its tail feathers. It's wearing plumes on its bum. It's going out to dinner."

"It's a kampat tiang to an Iban," said Siba, much amused at my expertise, "and to an Englishman it ought to be a Drongo. The old Iban like it, because it fights all the other birds and it's not afraid of eagles. And the uneducated Iban value strength and courage above all else."

We wound down the track along the side of the hill, past the penned pigs, and came to the huge longhouse. On the rough ground in front of the entrance steps an Iban blanket had been hung from a pole, its top stretched out on a cross-piece and its bottom end pulled out taut by two guy ropes, like a sail of a galleon. Its dyed, rich red-brown background was patterned with stylised frogs, fish, deer and crocodiles; and, beneath the large-headed figures of the spirits at its base, were woven four glasses, full of Guinness Stout.

Siba and Edward stopped and took off their watches. Leon removed the gold bangle from his wrist and put it in his pocket.

"You must remove your wedding ring, Redmond," said Siba, "an old man died when you were away on the Baleh and the longhouse is in mourning. Gold is taboo."

"We only have small party," said Leon. "No big parties for forty days. Then we drink tuak and all the girls cover their hand in black from the pot and they chase the mens they like. Very naughties."

At the top of the steps of his house apart, Dana's pet gibbon was waiting.

"Hello, and how are you?" said James.

The gibbon grimaced, shot up a main support pole, and shat with fright.

"He saw you first," I said.

We took off our shoes and entered Dana's big room. Inghai and Dana greeted us. We sat in a circle on the floor and Dana's eldest daughter brought us glasses and a kettle full of tuak on a tray.

We drank several glasses of tuak and then Dana insisted on an arm-wrestle with us all, lying flat out on the floor. Good manners dictate a win for your chief and host I reminded myself, loftily. But in the event there was not much choice: Dana could have taken my arm off at the elbow, I decided, as easily as you twist a wing from a roast chicken.

The victorious Dana led us into supper. Rings of bowls were laid out on the floor. Square yards of dishes were piled with roast babi and roast mouse-deer and chunks of thick pork fat. James looked upon the banquet, and smiled.

Dana spoke to Leon in Iban.

"Jams, my very good friend," said Leon, "the Tuai Rumah—he say he sorries there so little to eat."

"It's an heroic feast," said James.

"And you sit there," said Leon, pointing to a place with its own special bowl. I looked closer. It was a heap of rice and sebarau pieces.

James looked genuinely miserable.

"Ah, my very best friend," said Leon, putting an arm round his shoulders. "We jokes with you. Tonight you eat roast babi. Tonight you eat a meal you never forgets!"

Dana talked throughout the meal, Leon giving us *sotto voce* summaries of his address as it proceeded. It was the chief's report, the official history of the journey. He had greeted the Headmen of the following longhouses; he was sad to report that old so-and-so had died; someone else sent his respects to his parents-in-law; but for the bad cartridges sold by the Chinese we would have brought home many babi, and but for the love of the English for monkeys we would have brought them back, too; as it was we had killed monitor-lizard and turtle and preserved two basketfuls of fish; the upper Baleh was almost unreachable and when you got there the Kenyah had taken much good land; but the jungle was fresh and the water was clear and there were more fish and more babi than anyone could catch in a lifetime; we had not offended the spirits and they had raised the river when we asked them to do so; we had climbed above Bukit Batu Tiban and still we had found no trace of the Ukit; lastly, he must thank Jams and Redmon for the hunting trip and he felt bound to say that they *looked* strong and had behaved well but that they knew nothing of the river and nothing of the jungle.

"Badas!" concluded Dana. "Ngyrup!"

We then withdrew to the big room to drink arak; and the women took our places at the meal. I produced the Johnny Walker Black Label (much esteemed in the Far East) and we drank whisky. Pulling out the Polaroid I took everyone's picture, and group portraits of Dana's wife and daughters and grand-daughters.

We trooped off to call on one of Dana's sons-in-law who had just returned on leave from the Brunei oilfields, with some gin. We drank glasses of gin. We then descended the steps, very slowly, from Dana's dwelling to the main longhouse where we drank tuak and arak and orange squash and as much water as we could persuade Leon to give us, first with his family and some fifty visitors and then with Inghai's and fifty more. I think I showed Inghai how to use the Polaroid and he certainly dashed off with it delightedly, took everyone's picture and used up every box of film and every flashbulb.

We then crawled back up the hill to Dana's house, on hands and knees. Reaching the verandah I found myself staring into the little black face of the gibbon. We were on a level. He chattered excitedly, unafraid, plainly approving of this more normal mode of locomotion, a great improvement on the unnerving affectation of walking about standing up.

Dana said something to Leon.

"The Tuai Rumah," said Leon, "he wonch to know how many drinks."

"Whisky," said Siba.

"Arak," said Leon.

"Tuak," said Edward.

"Water," said Inghai.

"Orange," said I.

"Gin," said James. "Seven drinks."

"Seven drinks," said Dana triumphantly, in a perfect English accent, as he fell over the edge of his sleeping box and took a header into bed.

The next day we stirred at noon, found our own way, stiff and sullen, back to the hotel, and took a long siesta. In the evening Leon brought Thomas up to James's room and we went down to supper at the Chinese café.

Thomas was small, handsome, aloof. He wore shorts and a track-suit top and he thought a lot of himself. He came not from an enthusiastically democratic, free-and-easy Iban society, but from the rigidly structured, class-ridden Kayan. His smooth hands, excessive cleanliness, and, later, his refusal to help to carry any part of our baggage bespoke his status as a member of the maren, the chiefly class.

After supper, we all retired to James's room to plan the journey. On the final flight of stairs up to our floor young Iban boys were perched in silence, looking serious and expectant.

"They rot their spears tonight," announced Leon, hanging back in the corridor, mesmerised by the opportunity to risk a little rot on his own account as the enticing sound of pop music and laughter came through the door of the girls' room.

We pulled Leon in, sat down on James's bed and chair and table, spread out the maps, and talked business. A prau rather than a dugout would be needed. The Balui rapids could only be safely passed with the thrust of two large outboards each with its own driver.

"And what about the look-out in the bow?" said James to Thomas. "Will you do that?"

Thomas extinguished his half-smoked cigarette in the hotel ashtray, as fastidiously as if he had been wearing white gloves and was averse to dirtying their ends.

"No," said Thomas, "that is not my work."

For a bizarre moment I thought that James might be about to apologise for the *faux pas*, for having dared to suggest such a socially outrageous idea.

"So what is your work, in your opinion?"

"I shall be responsible for everything. We will visit one of my farms. I will introduce you to my own people, the Lahanna. We will have parties. We will have picnics."

"Picnics?" said James, taken aback, "picnics?"

"It is Kayan custom," said Leon. "Two longhouses make party together. The boys find the girls and the girls find the boys."

"Can Leon act as look-out?"

"No," said Thomas, "he doesn't know the river. I know a crew. The best. They take government officers. We will hire them in Belaga."

So we worked out the petrol we needed to reach Rumah Ukit, and the number of presents we must buy, the cigarettes and sarongs and salt and aginomoto, and the wages we must pay our crew; and the bill came to 3,050 dollars.

"Redmond," said James, "there is nothing to be done. We must auction Smythies."

Three days later, our supplies complete, our police passes in order, and the Rajang having risen high enough to allow a tong kang, a Chinese cargo boat, to negotiate the Pelagus rapids, we left the hotel at four in the morning and made our way down to the wharf. We took our places in the open hold amongst drums of petrol, two or three outboard motors, and cases of jeans and tee-shirts, Guinness Stout and cheap parangs, bound for the Belaga bazaar. The Chinese helmsman switched on the searchlight in the bow and revved up the shatteringly noisy diesel engine. The crew cast off from the jetty, the bow swung round into the current, and the tong kang or tin can began its slow, laborious, hammering voyage upstream.

The sun came up; the jungled banks of the wide, slow river edged monotonously by, hour after engine-pounding hour. The longhouses were large and semi-modernised, with concrete paths and corrugated iron roofs. We put in to most of them, picking up and dropping passengers — Iban back from Kapit market, having sold their joints of wild boar or mouse-deer or live turtles in sacks, Kayan completing their homeward journeys upstream. At every landing-stage a Chinese shopkeeper, the towkay in charge of the longhouse store, would be waiting, ready to exchange goods and dollars with our crew. In between whiles, James and I read Victor Hugo, Leon and Thomas slept, the duty helmsman manned the wheel in the small raised cabin-cum-bridge at the strern, and the off-duty Chinese gambled. They sat round a rectangular sheet of plywood balanced on the packing cases, slapping down their cards, scooping up their winnings, laughing and yelling whether fortune flashed them a nipple or poked them in the eye, besotted by chance, playing with an admirably sustained and concentrated passion.

I awoke with a violent twitch, convulsed by the blast of the boat's hooter. The helmsman, staring straight ahead with a seriousness which betokened him the owner of the craft, was summoning his gamblers to their duties. We were approaching the Pelagus rapids. The crew attended to the most important matters first, gathering up their now worn, marked, dirty, exhausted cards and flinging them overboard. They then checked the cargo lashings, hung out fenders, placed us evenly in the hold and took up positions fore and aft.

The tong kang juddered and slowed as we hit the first swirl of eddies. The helmsman opened up the diesel; we rounded a bend; and a large S-shaped course of fast water, compressed between clusters of rocks and filigreed with whirlpools, was revealed. The boat tossed and rolled; the Chinaman spun his helm; he alternately opened up and shut down his throttle, manoeuvring with great skill to keep to the centre of the current; and then we churned and thrashed and barrelled out into placid water again.

"Easies for him," said Leon with disdain. "Rich Chinaman. Big boat. Big engine. Not like the Baleh, eh Jams?"

"Many people have died here," said Thomas, defending the honour of his river.

Late in the evening we arrived at Belaga, a tiny market-town, an L-shaped street of shops with a Government rest house, an outlying school, a small hospital, a helicopter pad and a basketball court beside the river bank. We took rooms above a Chinese café, dined on mouse-deer, and watched squads of Chinese infants chasing locust-size cicadas with tiddler fishing nets on poles. The big green and black insects whirred into the lights, pulled their joy sticks the wrong way and knocked themselves out on the ceiling, mixed up their flaps and powered into the shelf of baked bean tins, forgot to readjust their ailerons and splashed down in James's beer. At every misfortune the cicadas clicked like clockwork toys on the move. James picked up his captive, his finger and thumb on its abdomen, and it protested with a burst of sound like a football rattle.

"They good to eat," said Leon, "they taste like little fishes."

"No more little fishes. Not this week," said James, releasing the cicada.

The next morning we carried our Bergens down to the jetty, where our boat was waiting. It was a wide, capacious dugout with high sides, an awning in the centre and a raised, roofed platform behind it for the two helmsmen. Two powerful outboards with long handles were mounted in the stern. The Kayan boatman was the first fat man we had seen in Borneo, which was a bad sign. And worse, one of the petrol drums had been decanted into suspiciously few smaller vessels.

The second driver, the boatman's son, was equally bloated. Maybe, I comforted myself, they had not grown fat on stolen petrol exchanged for seven legs of pork and lots of crackling every week of their lives, but were simply the direct descendants of Kam Diam, whom Beccari met in Belaga in 1866: "chief of one of the nearest villages on the Baloi [Balui] . . . He was unlike any of the Kayans, or even Dyaks I had yet seen, and was certainly the stoutest and fattest man I ever saw in Borneo."

"We've been conned already," said James, looking like a very old bloodhound. "Shall we fight them to the death *now*, or shall we wait until they do something *really unforgivable?*"

"I rather think we ought to take this slowly," I said. "Kayan karate is probably wonderful to watch, and they're supposed to be the best wrestlers in Borneo. But don't let me stop you. When you reach my age you'll realise that there are occasions—just a few—when, painful though it may be, one must step aside and give the young a chance."

"He's not in on it, anyhow," said James, pointing at the bow look-out, who was casting off. Thin, mournful, scraggy, silent, the Kayan look-out sat in the bow, cross-legged, his back to us, watching the current as the engines started and we surged upstream. His ear-lobes were looped and the top flaps of his ears were pierced with holes large enough to take a boar's tusk apiece. Looking through his ears from behind, you could see the trees on either river bank ahead.

"Silly old loopy-lugs," said James, venting his annoyance.

We were now well into Kayan country, the land of the Borneo tribes whom Hose admired most of all: "They are a warlike people, but less truculent than the Sea Dyaks, more staid and conservative and religious, and less sociable. They do not wantonly enter into quarrels; they respect and obey their chiefs. They are equally industrious with the Sea Dyaks, and though somewhat slow and heavy in both mind and body, they are more skilled in the handicrafts than any of the other peoples."

We called in at Long Murum to eat our lunch of pork and rice, to buy more wild pig and more rice, to admire the modern longhouse, and to wait while Thomas discussed probable, possible and fantastic compensation payments which the government might make should Long Murum and its farms be flooded to make the great lake. Thomas, as a maren, was entitled to receive so many days' work from the panyin and hipuy of his people, the Lahannan Kayan, that he was free to live a life of leisure, or to engage in politics, or to trade with the nomads on his own account, or to enjoy appropriating James and me and Leon and our boat and crew for his private Royal Progress up his own river.

The panyin and hipuy, the commoners of the Kayan longhouse, are not allowed to leave it unless the chief gives his permission, but there is also a fourth class, the lowliest of all, the dipen, the slaves. Descendants of other tribes or peoples captured in war or by raiding parties, the dipen themselves fall into two categories: servants who live in the master's household and the lucky few who have been permitted to set up house on their own. Although their owner no longer arranges their marriages and disposes their children where he will, living-in dipen can never work for themselves. Slaves with their own rooms or their own farms, however, can theoretically manage a few unindebted days on their fields if their health lasts—and once they have fulfilled their obligations to the chief and to their maren master.

After a stop for Guinness Stout in another modern longhouse which had its egg-holding offering-sticks to Bungan set in rows above the landing stage, Thomas took us to visit such a family. At least I think he did—the smallholding consisted of a well-kept pepper plantation, a tiny two-room longhouse and a cluster of storage huts. Thomas insisted that it was all his land and his buildings; but when, on the jetty, I asked Leon if this was a settlement of dipen, Leon stopped me.

"Redmon," he said, lowering his voice, taking my arm and holding me back, "these not our peoples. We guests here, my friend. That word you use—you read it in a book, eh?"

"Yes, I did. I read it in Victor King's *Essays on Borneo Societies*. He says the Kayan keep slaves and that the Iban are the randiest race on earth."

"No, my friend," said Leon, "I not jokes with you. You *never* use that word. Everyone know who is dipen. Everyone know the mothers and fathers of all the people, but you never tell to them. These poor people—maybe. I not know. These Thomas friends. These good people. We their guests."

After a glass of tuak and a cheroot of Kayan tobacco wrapped in banana leaf with Thomas's tenant farmers, who treated him with extreme deference, we set off upriver again. The Balui was still wide and slow and much frequented by praus. There were no eagles, no herons, very few kingfishers; and all day long we had seen only one pair of hornbills.

That evening we reached Rumah Lahannan. The path from the landing-place led past a half-constructed prau (its clinker sides being built up on the hollowed tree-trunk hull), wound amongst padi storage huts, beneath coconut palms, a kapok tree, and, a modern improvement, a row of pig pens. The longhouse itself was large, well built, populous and busy. A schoolhouse, complete with playing fields and a flag pole, stood on the opposite bank.

We were greeted by Thomas's parents; and by his very pretty, unmarried sister. Thomas went off to visit his friends in their amins (the Kayan word for bilek) and his sister, having served us a meal of fish and rice, showed us to our sleeping quarters, a separate room adjacent to the family's own amin and complete with a kitchen-shed on stilts to the rear. The community itself was rich enough to pump water from the river with an electric motor and petrol-driven generator to a longhouse tank whence pipes ran to each household. We filled our water bottles from the kitchen tap, and laid out our sleeping equipment round the edge of the split-bamboo floor, a rolled-shirt pillow in each place. Thomas's sister was annoyingly attentive to Leon.

"Have you eaten enough?" she asked in excellent English. "Will you be comfortable here?"

"I not knows yet," said Leon, cheering up, beginning to swagger, testing the floor with his foot as if he was only used to sleeping between silk sheets in a feather bed.

"Will you have coffee?" said the girl, anxious, slight, watching him with her big brown eyes and shaking her long hair back over her shoulders with a toss of the head. "We have a little coffee."

"Later," said Leon, going to his padi-basket, squatting down with an exaggerated flexing of the outsize muscles in his legs and thighs, pulling out his watch and strapping it on. "We take coffees later. Now we take a bath. Then we make play and sing songs. Then I tell you. If I not sleeps, I come and tell you."

The girl put her right hand over her eyes, giggled, spun round on her bare feet, lifted her sarong with her left hand, stepped over the sill of the door, and disappeared. Leon grinned, his old self restored.

"Wasn't that over-egging the pudding?" said James.

"Pudding?" said Leon.

"Wasn't that over the top? Weren't you a bit forward? Didn't you come on a bit strong?"

"She like me," said Leon, beaming, unpacking a clean white tee-shirt with Guinness Stout printed on the front and holding it up for our admiration.

"You embarrassed the young lady."

"Jams, Jams, my best friend," said Leon, unfurling a pair of long brown trousers and picking up a towel. "Now we take a bath in the river. We soaps. Tonight we find you Kayan girl." Leon edged towards the door.

"We find you wise girl who not sillies."

Leon paused in the doorway.

"We find you old Kayan girl. We find you Kayan girl so old she have no tooths. We find you Kayan girl so wise she have no hair. We find you widow! We find you grandmother!"

Leon, howling with laughter, slammed the door and ran off down the verandah. James picked up a towel, knotted it, and dashed out after him. It was going to be an active night.

Fresh from a swim and dressed in clean clothes, I tried to take a sleep on my patch of floor, but the ominous noise of a gathering crowd in the amin next door precluded such an escape. Would we have to sing? Would I be forced to try the nagdjat, the most excruciatingly painful dance on earth, all over again? Would a striptease be acceptable, instead?

Thomas's sister came to summon us. She was wearing a dark-green folded-down sarong; and a white tee-shirt which stretched tight across her flat stomach and delineated her small breasts and perky nipples with a loving care for detail.

"My mother has made coffee," she said. And, to Leon, "Will you dance later? An Iban dance?"

"You ask," said Leon, grinning stupidly at James, "I do anythings."

The amin was full of people and the air was dense with smoke and noise. Men and women leant against the walls and sat cross-legged in concentric circles on the floor. Children ran in and out, fell over each other, perched on their parents' legs. Thomas's sister showed us to our places in the middle of the room. We sat and drank our thick, sweet coffee, and then jugs of tuak were brought. Young girls put Kayan cheroots in our mouths and lit them. Thomas produced a bottle of whisky from our stores and the boatman and his son handed round cans from our crate of Guinness.

An intelligent-looking woman, perhaps in her thirties, with a young girl at her side, knelt in front of me. The hubbub petered out into silence. The woman looked at the floor, concentrated, and then began to sing, her voice high-pitched, her body swaying with the effort.

"She welcomes you," whispered Thomas, sitting to my right, "she says you have come all the way from England, at the far end of the earth; she says you come from a land beyond the river and yet you have found your way to our poor longhouse."

The poet finished her verse, and the sound was immediately resolved in a deep, long-drawn-out cadence sung by all the men in the room before she resumed her powerful, clear monotone.

"She tells of the heroes of this place," said Thomas, "and when she ends her story you must drink the tuak she will give you, all in one go."

"We've just walked into Homer, and sat down inside," hissed James, much excited.

The song ended. The chorus reverberated in the wooden room.

I took the half-pint glass of tuak and emptied it, one gulp ahead of choking, all the way. The men roared their approval.

The poet and her understudy, still kneeling, shuffled in front of James. The poets faced each other. The two women then gave each other half a giggle and launched into an obviously prepared duet. Everyone laughed and clapped at once, the high chant hanging precise above the chaos of noise.

"She never went to school," said Thomas, "but she is very witty. She is famous amongst all the Kayan. We Lahannan have a clever singer of songs. She says that James is bald, like the chief of the gods. But perhaps he is a mountain, like Kinabalu? Because all the hairs on his head, like the trees on a mountian, found it too hard to live so near to the sky and so one day they all ran down together and took shelter under his chin, and one or two, who could not run so fast, hid under his nose."

James drank his tuak with professional ease and, to the general applause, everyone else drank theirs, or the nearest can of Guinness, or took a slug from the whisky bottle. The pair of singers then moved in front of Leon, who looked uneasy. The song and chorus began again, to the same notes.

"She welcomes Leon, too, but for him it is different," said Thomas. "She says he is welcome because he comes in peace, without his spear and without the guns the Rajah gave to him. We are all one people now. We must forget our differences. The war is over. And now she says he must forgive the song, too, because the singer is drunk. They are not her words."

The last chorus resounded, shaking the bamboo floor.

"What war? What are you talking about?" I said.

"Not now," said Thomas sharply, getting to his feet. "I tell you another time."

The party broke up into small groups. Loopy-lugs, for some reason, having purloined a kettle-full of tuak, came and sat opposite me. He poured two glasses, checked the levels, clinked them together, offered me one and took the other. We were engaged, I realised with dismay, in a drinking contest.

Four glasses later, the ears of our bow look-out had turned as red as tulips and the holes in their shells seemed to be jiggling about, describing little circles of their own. It was time to stop. I placed my re-filled glass in front of him, indicating abject surrender. Loopy-lugs bared his misshapen teeth in a smile, drained both glasses, smacked his lips, shook my hand, lay full length on the floor for a second or two, and then jumped to his feet and left the room as if his evening was only just beginning.

I undid my crossed legs, rubbed some feeling back into my calves and ankles, and got up, very slowly. I walked up the two planks I was on, negotiated a pack of children sitting on the calm point above the fulcrum, and then, as the see-saw tipped the other way, I shot out of the door and fetched up against the rail of the verandah. A smart young Kayan held my arm, firmly.

"Good evening," he said, in excellent English, "have you come to take the air?"

"Yes, I suppose I have," I said, gasping it in.

He found my hand and shook it.

"How do you do? I'm what you might call the village schoolmaster."

"You teach over there?" I said stupidly, pointing into the dark at the opposite bank, "in the school?"

"That's right," he said, kindly, "but I sleep here in the longhouse. I'm a Kayan. I trained in Kuching, but after college we all have to teach for a year up-country. I think it's a good plan, don't you? Did you train anywhere?"

"Yes, I trained in Oxford."

The schoolmaster turned round, leaned against the rail beside me, and stared into the tropical night.

"I would have loved to go to Oxford," he said, with passion. "For me, it would be the celestial city. And, just think, my friend, two or three years ago, a mere two or three years ago, I might have had the chance. I'd have worked at my studies, all day long. And I might have passed out top and won a scholarship. But now England has no money and Mrs Thatcher cannot afford us. Our government was angry, my friend, very angry, when she said no more of us could go to your universities. You tell her—it was not wise. In time, we will forget your country. Soon, no English will be taught in our schools. Only Bahasa. The whole of Malaysia will become Muslim. Already, to spite you, our government buys its cars, its police vehicles, its ships, from Japan—and now we are to let them build a dam here."

"I am sorry," I said, "but we are not rich any more."

"No, my friend, it's not riches, it's an attitude. You decided to have no more to do with us. What's a scholarship here and there? And yet it kept all our young teachers happy, the thought of it."

166

Further up the longhouse verandah, in a circle of light cast by a kerosene lamp slung from a rafter, James and Leon sat intent in the middle of a group of young men and girls. A beautiful lilting song began.

"You see," said my sad companion, "even the songs are in Bahasa Malay. This one is an old custom. The missionaries tried to stop it. The girl sings a verse and then the boy. You must make it up as you go along. If the words don't rhyme or you can't find anything to say, you must take something off. The girls wear more trinkets, so they have an advantage. But the boys try harder, because they love to see the girls undress. And some girls, my friend, they just make-believe they have nothing to say, that they have run out of verses, because they love the boys to watch them as they undress. But, let me tell you, it's the quickest way to teach a new language. My pupils learn fast. I turn them all into poets. Every one."

The tuak still playing in my stomach, milk-churning itself into butter, I decided, on the whole, that perhaps I would not join the young things just yet, that maybe it would be fairer to wait a while, to wait, say, until James had lost his trousers.

"In the welcome song that the woman sang to us," I said, "Thomas told me she sang about the war. She said that Leon was a friend now, that the war was over. Did some of the Iban join the Japs? What happened?"

"Oh no—you've got it all wrong," said the schoolmaster, turning back to lean on the rail and look out into the dark. "When Harrisson and the English and the Australians parachuted into the central uplands, the Kelabit country, the Kelabits joined them, and then the Kayan, and then the Iban, and we all killed the Japanese together. But that was just a skirmish. It came and it went. For us, the real war took place in 1863. The Iban had been migrating towards our lands for years, taking heads, attacking all the weak tribes, raiding against the Melanau peoples in the Rajang. As far as we were concerned, the English fought for the Iban and not the other way about. And as for the Melanau, if they owed allegiance to anyone, it was to the Rajahs of Brunei. So in 1859 they killed two of your Rajah James Brooke's men at Kanowit, Charles Fox and Henry Steele. They thought it would teach him a lesson, that the Iban and the English would go away, that they would leave us alone. But you didn't go away; and so Sawing and Sakalai and Talip, the Melanau chiefs from Kanowit, went to hide with their people on the Rajang; and they thought they would be safe. But the Iban and the English waited. You waited for five years.

"And then Charles Brooke, the second English Rajah, came against us. He armed the Iban and his own Malays with guns—and he came against us with fifteen thousand men in five hundred war canoes. He was a terrible, cruel, silent man, my friend—whatever your history books may say. He let the Iban kill the Melanau—he let them burn down the longhouses and the padi stores; he let them steal all their ancient jars and gongs; he let them take the heads of the warriors, and their wives, and their children. It was the greatest slaughter that Borneo has ever seen. The Melanau chiefs came to us for safety. They came to us for their lives and we promised to protect them. But what could we do? How could we fight against guns, with the spear and the blowpipe? Even in the jungle, your Charles Brooke was impossible to ambush. He fought like a bird. He placed his army like a bird—he walked in the centre with his new guns and his Malays, the eyes and the beak, and the Ibans beat forward like the outstretched wings of the kite and our warriors were caught from all sides and their heads were cut off. So we moved back behind the Pelagus rapids, and then we escaped beyond the Bakun rapids, and we lost all our rich lands on the upper Rajang, and this part of the river was re-named the Balui. But that was not the end of it—your Rajah sent a captive Kayan to us with his flag, and a cannon ball. He sent them to a great Kayan chief, Oyong Hang. If we sent back the flag, we could make peace with the Iban. If we sent back the cannon ball, Charles Brooke would come again. Oyong Hang, unlike your Rajah, my good friend, was a real leader of men. He knew he must do his own filthy work and not ask the Iban to do it for him. He refused to disgrace his own warriors; and he refused to let any more of our women and our children die. So he called a meeting of all the Kayan. And at the meeting, he asked Chief Sakalai and Talip to come to him. They knelt before him, knowing what he had to do, these men who had come to us for their lives, trusting to our protection. In front of everyone, he drew his parang. He cut off their heads. He sent their heads to your Rajah. He returned the flag. Later, he sent Chief Sawing, too, thinking he might be spared. But your Rajah had him killed, by a Malay. The Malay pushed a kris between his shoulders, into his heart. So there you are my friend—that is why the woman sang her song to the Iban. The Iban are settled on our lands, and on the lands of the Melanau. Silly, isn't it? As she says, it is all a long time ago. In fact it is one hundred and twenty years ago. And we have not forgotten. And we never will."

The lilting song continued, each verse ending in shrieks of laughter. James and Leon had lost their shirts and there was a bracelet or two on the floor in front of each girl. The lamp above their heads, swayed by the stamping and clapping, cast lines of shadow from the roof-support poles out across the pig pen and the padi storage huts, threw pendulate stripes of darkness over a clump of bamboo and up the boles of the coconut palms. Gradually, the light seemed to come to rest, and, in its place, the longhouse began, very gently, to swing, back and forth, in the night air.

"Are you all right?" said the schoolmaster, his voice unaccountably muffled and his head, for no reason, dancing softly on his shoulders.

"No, I'm not, thank you. I believe I must be drunk. I think I'm going to be sick."

"I'm drunk, too," he said, affably. "In fact everybody is drunk. I've had tuak and arak and whisky and Guinness Stout. It's no reason to stop talking, just because you're drunk. We are having a serious conversation."

"I know we are."

"We are educated men," he said, gripping my arm and jerking it up and down for emphasis, "being drunk does not alter the fact. We are discussing the history of our countries and I believe we should continue to do so."

"I'm going to be sick."

"Of course you are. We are all sick when we drink too much. But my dear friend, I beg you not to take it so seriously."

"Please. Where can I go to be sick?"

"Over there," he said pointing with his free arm towards the dark end of the verandah, away from the revellers. "If you insist on stopping our exchange of ideas, I will join the singers, if you don't mind? You see—on that bank" (he gestured across the river) "I am an old schoolmaster, but on this bank I am a young Kayan. I, too, like to see the girls undress. I will tell the others—you will join us later, and sing. Be sick over the edge. That's what I do. And you'll notice, in the morning, that the chickens have pecked it all up. Kayan chickens, my friend, are very fond of tuak."

I hung on to the rail and groped my way down to the far end of the longhouse. I sat on the edge of the platform, clear of the padi-drying apron, and began to be sick. On the fourteenth retch, in spasm from my duodenum to my oesophagus, wondering vaguely if the intermittent current would carry my epiglottis clear away, I felt something push against my back. It was an old dog. He was perhaps not feeling too good himself. He settled down beside me and put his head on my thighs. He was mangy and dusty and his fur was rough to stroke. I lay back on the boards for a moment, and fell asleep.

· SEVENTEEN ·

I awoke just before dawn, my head resting on the old dog's neck. Someone seemed to have inserted a pestle into my cerebellum during the night, and was now using the inside top of my skull as a mortar. The dog got up, shook his own head, stretched, and hobbled off down the verandah. I set off slowly to look for our door, remembered it by its broken wooden latch, and found my Bergen where I had left it against the wall. James was curled up snoring, but Leon's place was empty. I undid the medicine bag as quietly as I could, took three codeine phosphate pills, put four Alka-seltzer in my mess-tin and emptied my water bottle on top of them. I let the fizz dish-wash away the puke-crust on my teeth and then went to re-fill the flask from the tap. A cock crowed.

Behind the wooden partition that separated the kitchen from the rest of the room Leon was flat on his back on the floor, asleep. Beside him and across him lay Thomas's sister, her head on his chest, her long black hair splayed over his crude tattoos. Her right arm stretched up to his left shoulder, her thigh rested over his genitals. They were breathing deeply, in rhythm with each other. Even their clothes looked happy; the green sarong and Leon's new tee-shirt and trousers were entangled together in a pile at their feet. I stood for a moment, looking at the brown curl of the girl's back, the dip of her thin shoulders, at her right breast squashed against Leon's ribs, at the long triangle of her legs and the rounded curves and hollows of her muscled buttocks, at a scar at the back of her right knee. And then I crept away, feeling like the oldest voyeur in the world, punished with a headache which even I did not deserve; and I decided to go for a swim and to fill my water bottle in the river.

After breakfast, the Kayan girls and boys and their schoolmaster, in a fleet of canoes, set off across the river to school, and we set off to find the Ukit.

The bank-side hills grew steeper, the jungle richer, but there was still little sign of bird life. Loopy-lugs, insultingly unaffected by our drinking contest, perched in the bow. The fat drivers, father and son, manned the outboards in the stern. James and I settled to reading *Les Misérables* under the awning, and Leon and Thomas slept.

We stopped for our lunch of pork and rice at a Kayan longhouse which was luxuriously equipped with raised pathways of wooden planking between the storage huts, a Chinese shop, and a racing war-canoe slung from the rafters of the verandah—a possible winner at the next Belaga regatta and a memorial of Hose's great peacemaking ceremony of 1899, when formerly hostile tribes raced each other, in boats carrying seventy warriors apiece, down a four-mile stretch of the Baram.

Leon, uncharacteristically quiet, sat apart from the others, and I joined him.

"So what happened last night?" I said.

"You got drunks," said Leon, pushing a cube of pork fat into his mouth with his fingers, "you got drunks like a man who still lives in his mother's room. You got drunks like a schoolboy. You made noises like a babi when he looks in the ground for foods."

"I expect you made a bit of noise yourself."

"Eh? Whassit?"

"After the singing."

"James won all the songs. The girls—they make him take his shirt off, but then he make them take off all their bangles. They very young, very sillies, very beautifuls. I lose. Malay song, very difficult. We got drunks, too. I lose my trousers, but I keep my pants."

"All night long? You sure?"

"Where you sleeps Redmon?" said Leon, starting to grin, taking an outsize scoop of rice in one hand and another half-cooked lump of globby pig in the other. "Where you sleeps?"

"I slept on the ruai; and then I came to get a little water from the tap."

"From the tap, eh? I thought you never look in the kitchen. I thought we safe. But we not. You make noise like a babi and you have noses like a dog. She very naughty girl. She not sleeps. She come and tell me. She say some words to me. She like me very much."

"You're a hell of a guy—but it's your watch they like."

"If I find Ukit girl," said Leon, dribbling pork fat from both ends of a ten-inch grin, "if Ukit girl she like me very much, then we go to the boat—and I take her to Belaga, and then to Kapit, and then to Sibu, and then to the seas; and there we have peaces together well away from Redmon."

Later that afternoon, we reached Rumah Ukit. Ramshackle steps led up the bank from the landing area and a young Ukit stood at the top. He was smartly dressed in cotton trousers and a tee-shirt, but even so he was quite different from any of the Borneo people we had met. He was smaller, paler, more alert; his eyes were enormous. And he took me by the arm.

"Could you please already actually, sir," he said, "teach us the seven-step disco?"

"I've never been to a disco."

"No sir," he said, staring intently into my eyes, "you actually do not understand me. We believe here that seven is the latest step."

At that moment, James, carrying his Bergen on his back, came up the stairway, followed by Leon and Thomas.

"Good afternoon," said James, "and what seems to be the trouble?"

"Actually, sir," said the Ukit, "you, too, can teach us the seven-step disco—if you don't mind."

"I've never been to a disco," said James, wheezing through his beard with surprise.

"That does not seem to be the point at issue," I said. "And anyway you'd probably be *tremendous*."

"Jams," said Leon to the Ukit, confidentially, "he not tell you—but he the greatest poet in all Inglang. He know all the songs. He know all the dances. That's what he do all day."

"Well then, sir, that is actually settled," said the Ukit. "You will stay with my sister and you will teach us the seven-step disco. We will eat, and we will have games. We have already a tape of music and we have a recorder. You have batteries?"

"We have the best battery in the world," said Leon with pride. "We have battery from the army of Inglang."

"Then sir, perhaps already you will follow me?" said the Ukit.

Government-sponsored or not, Rumah Ukit was not a substantial settlement in Iban or Kenyah or Kayan terms. There were very few padi-storage huts (and probably very little padi was being grown). The longhouse itself, despite its novel window-frames, its corrugated-iron roof and its imported machine-made planking, looked half-abandoned. It was split into several sections, and smaller dwellings, here and there, perched on their own stilts. The hunter-gatherer Ukit, plainly, had not taken to the settled life of the farmer, even the occasionally nomadic life of the shifting cultivation of hill rice. He might come to Rumah Ukit to trade his produce—wild pig, deer, sago or camphor—or to set up a temporary room so that his children might be sent to school in Belaga, but his mind and his extraordinary skills were obviously still exercised where they always had been, in deep primary jungle.

A small group of girls who were sitting under a hut, weaving rattan mats in the shade, waved at us, shouted, and giggled.

"Ukit girl," said Leon, sticking out his chest and adjusting his ridiculous pork-pie-cum-Homburg hat.

"The Ukit make the best mats in Borneo," said Thomas. "This evening they will cook for us at the picnic."

"Will you take all of us young people on a picnic, actually?" said our Ukit guide.

"Certainly," said James.

We walked over to the girls. Our Ukit passed on the news. The girls laughed and began rolling up their mats. The smallest and prettiest, as big-eyed as a hare in short grass, scrutinised James.

"You make baby here?" she asked.

"Not until after tea," said James, giving his beard a bemused tug with his right hand.

"You teach us English?" she persisted. "You stay?"

"Okey-scrokes," said James.

The girl assumed an air of extreme puzzlement, frowning, tossing her head to shake the long black hair away from her eyes.

"What you call that?" she said suddenly, pointing, as I thought, straight at my crutch.

"What's wrong with it?" I said, looking down at once, aghast.

"Everything," said James, shutting his eyes, covering them with his hand, and shaking with laughter until his Bergen jiggled about.

"Legs," said Leon, "it's called a legs."

"You have dollars for Three Legs?" said the girl, brightening.

"What?" I said, transfixed.

"It's a powder," said Thomas, "a powder for headaches which the Chinese sell. They ask for it here, all the time."

"Jesus," spluttered James, "Redmond thought they were after his third leg."

"Actually sir," said our guide, "would you follow me? I will show you where you sleep. Then I will tell my friends. And then I will bring the recorder to you and you may give us your batteries, if you please?"

We climbed a sapling-thin notched pole, fifteen feet up, to a small series of huts set in front and to the side of the main longhouse. A girl, perhaps in her twenties, greeted us. Much shaken, I made straight for a safe corner in which to dump my reassuring Bergen.

"Poor old Redmond," said James, still skittish, "cheer up—soon you make disco and then you make baby."

"Redmon!" said Leon, joining in, "he make new dance! he fall over his feet!"

"I will not sleep here," announced Thomas, unsmiling, "I will sleep in the Headman's room."

"Hang on," said James, "isn't that *serious* bad manners? Shouldn't we sleep in the Headman's room? And why haven't we been taken to pay our respects to him, anyway? And what about all those presents for him?"

"I will look after the presents," said Thomas, with a smirk. "You don't worry about a thing. You just enjoy yourself."

"I *am* beginning to worry," said James. "What's going on?"

"Please sir," said our guide, distressed, "you stay here. We are all young here. Do not stay with the old men. We laugh at them."

"Laugh at them? Why?" said James.

"Because they are old," said our guide. "And also, actually, because they are ignorant. They believe that the earth is flat, whereas it is round, like a ball. But now sir you will come with me, and we will make picnic."

We edged our way backwards down the long spindly pole and took a different path through the settlement. Behind one hut a middle-aged woman was fanning a small fire, preparing a lime paste which is then spread on a banana leaf and wrapped round half a betel nut for more piquant chewing. Beneath another, a youngish Ukit was running a strip of rattan through a newly made blowpipe, and checking his bore-polishing, at intervals, by holding the seven-foot length of hardwood up against the light and squinting down the tube as one might check the shine in a shotgun barrel.

Five girls and four boys had assembled by the prau. Thomas fetched our fat drivers and Loopy-lugs from their quarters in the main longhouse and we motored upstream to a shingle promontory. The girls cooked rice and the roast babi and James interrogated the boys.

"What do you do all day?" he asked our guide. "Are you still at school?"

"No sir, I have actually left school," said the Ukit, lobbing pebbles, with unnerving accuracy, at a half-submerged rock in the river. "I do nothing. The old men say that I and my friends should grow padi; or we must go with them in the jungle, and find camphor, and hunt animals with the blowpipe. But I wish to go to work in a timber camp, or to Europe. I would like, sir, to visit your disco."

"Have you been to a disco?"

"No sir, but I believe there to be a disco in Kuching."

"Have you been to Kuching?"

"No sir, none of us have been to Kuching. We have been to Belaga, to the school."

"The Ukit man," said Leon, "he the greatest hunter of camphor. He know when to cut the camphor tree. He dream of girls and he have good lucks. He not smoke and then he find the trees. He cut it—one, two, three cuts. He take out the side of the tree. He scrape it all out. But sometimes it not hard. Sometimes he cut the tree and it all white and stick on his fingers like the juice from his spear. Then he run home and kill his wife. It mean she have other mens. Is true."

"No sir, it is not true," said the young Ukit, much affronted. "You are wrong. We are educated men. We do not believe it. Only the old men here believe it. They are all stupid. And that is why, actually, we have decided not to go with them. They also think the sky fits on the earth, like an upturned cooking pot. They are wrong."

"They are probably right about lots of other things," said James, "about all kinds of things that matter just as much."

"We do not think so," said the young Ukit, and his companions nodded their agreement.

"Tomorrow we will have a very large picnic," said Thomas, as the girls joined us with the food. "Tomorrow we will make many trips to Rumah Daro, and bring all the young Kayan here."

Back at the hut Leon fitted our army batteries into the cassette player and the machine came horribly to life. The tape of pop music sounded over-excited about some small domestic problem in the usual kind of way.

Thomas went off to issue invitations to the party. James made for a corner of the room, sat down, and wedged himself in. Leon lay flat on the floor and refused to move. The nine young Ukits, and our hostess, encircled me.

"Please sir," said our guide, grabbing my arm with quite unnecessary force, "you will already teach us the seven-step disco?"

"I can't do it," I said, smiling serenely, "but James is a *wonderful dancer*. He knows all the dances. He is the best dancer in all England. That's what he does all day. He can pirouette on a cotton reel. He does *everything*."

"I've got a bad leg," said James.

"No sir," said the Ukit to me, "I actually think you do not understand us. We wish to learn the seven-step disco."

Leon began to giggle.

"You ask Leon," I said, trying to inch towards my corner, "he'll teach you. He'll teach all the girls."

"I very old. I very tireds. Now I sleeps," said Leon, shutting his eyes and grinning his most stupid grin.

"That's right," said James, pulling his Bergen in front of him, barricading himself in, "he is very tired."

"You see sir," said the Ukit, "your friends are actually not to be disturbed. They actually tell us already that you are the chief of the seven-step disco. In Europe, you win prizes."

Leon began to roll about on the floor. It was a plot.

"You bastards!" I said.

"Come come," said James.

"Now nows," said Leon.

The group of Ukit unhanded me and stood back, concentrating. There was nothing for it.

"I got you by the short and curlies, baby," sang the popstar, or something of the sort. I lifted my legs, alternately. I raised my right arm, twirled it about a bit, and then, with outstretched finger, pointed out the exact positions of mosquitoes on an imaginary ceiling. This process I repeated with my left arm. I then, with extreme difficulty, combined all these motor manifestations of imminent nervous collapse, and, inspired, I added further evidence of backfiring synapses, shaking my head like the front end of a sheepdog back from a swim. The Ukit mimicked every movement, perfectly. And so it was that the seven-step paraplegic wobble came to central Borneo.

"If that disco dance," said Leon, sitting up, "it damn sillies."

"The trick is," said James, "to keep it up all night."

We took out three bottles of whisky from the Bergen store and sent Leon off to the Chinese shop to buy six crates of Guinness Stout. The young Ukit were bouncing up and down, entirely unassisted. It began to seem possible that we might enjoy the evening. Our hostess lit two kerosene lamps which hung from the rafters.

Older members of the tribe began to arrive, crowding on to the small wooden platform outside the door and peering in at the extraordinary antics of their educated relations.

"If you like," said our guide, "you must ask the old people to join our party. It is the custom."

So we ushered in our guests, and they sat round the walls, their backs against the planking and their legs straight out in front of them. Leon, with a lot of help, eventually ferried all the Guinness up the pole and distributed the bottles. The old women, their breasts long and wrinkled as if soaked in formalin but their eyes still bright, clutched their half-pints with one hand and pulled their betel-nut boxes and cheroot tins out of their skirts with the other. The old men passed round the whisky. The room began to fill with acrid smoke.

Leon picked out the prettiest young Ukit and engaged her in the paraplegic wobble. Our guide, himself tiring of the dance, came and sat beside us.

"Where do your people come from?" said James. "Have you always lived here?"

"No thank you sir," said the Ukit, "we moved to the Kayan lands, in the war."

"What war?"

"The great war, when the Iban from Kapit came up the Baleh to take our heads. When the Iban fought the Kayan."

"And were you nomads then? Have you always been nomads?"

"Sir, we are educated. But our fathers are nomads. Many of our people are still nomads. They live in the jungle. They make shelters of leaves in the jungle and they go hunting until they have killed all the old pigs and all the old monkeys within a day's walk, or two, or three. Then they move on. They never kill too many of the wives of the pigs or the monkeys, not like the Iban. So they always have enough to eat. They know how to live in the jungle. Sometimes they go to Kalimantan. They go everywhere. But it is very hard, very ignorant. It is not for us."

The young Ukit took a long pull on his cheroot, exhaled with a great sigh, and then fixed James with his enormous, bulging, intense eyes.

"Would I find a job in your country, James? Would I find a job in England? Would I?"

"It is very difficult," said James, taken aback, "there are not enough jobs in our country either. There are not enough jobs to go round."

At that moment, from outside, there came a long, wailing scream, followed by a series of sharp, shrill cries. Several of the women sprang up and disappeared out of the door; Leon unhooked a lamp, and James and I followed him on to the platform. Below us, the women were already tending someone who was lying on the ground, moaning. We clambered down and joined the circle. A young woman, stretched out on her back in the refuse and the pig shit, was tossing her head from side to side, muttering to herself and holding her sides with her hands.

"She's in terrible pain," said James, peering at her distorted features. "She must have fallen off that filthy pole. She's probably smashed her ribs."

One of the women knelt down and held the frantic head in her lap.

"Get the DF 118s", said James, "and tell someone who speaks English to get down here. And turn that filthy noise off."

"What about the morphine?" I said.

"No, Redmond, I know you're dying to use it. But you've never done it before. You'd probably kill her."

I got back up the pole, grabbed our guide, found the painkillers and switched off the cassette recorder. By the time I reached the ground, someone had switched it on again.

James took the packet of pills, gave two to the woman, produced a bottle of Guinness from his trouser pocket, opened it with a drinker's attachment on his penknife, and held the woman's head as she swallowed. Four women then carried her across the compound to a lone hut on the far side. An old man watched impassively as the wounded woman was lowered into her sleeping box.

"Tell him," said James, "to give her two more of these when she wakes up. And tell him—if she's no better in the morning we'll take her to hospital in Belaga."

We left our guide with the women and made our way back to the party. The dancing and drinking was wilder than before, and the music sounded many decibels louder. The girls insisted we do the wobble with them.

Our guide returned. We took him to our corner and sat down.

"Well?" said James, "how is she? What do you think happened?"

"She says her bones hurt here," said the Ukit, rubbing his ribs, "she says the medicine you gave her is very good, very strong. The old women send me away, sir. They say, actually, that she is now having a baby. It should stay inside. But it is coming out. There is now very much blood, I think."

"Christ," said James, "then we will leave for Belaga in the morning.'

"You must not do that," said the Ukit, "it is not your affair. It is not your business."

"Why not? What do you mean?"

"Well sir, you actually promised that you would take us for a picnic tomorrow."

"But, she might be *dying*," said James, astonished.

"You made a promise to us," said the Ukit, stubbornly, "you must keep your promise."

"But can't you see that all that's changed?" said James, his arms crooked in front of him, his palms upturned for emphasis. "She fell coming to *our* party. She is *our* responsibility. We must save her life. It's simple."

"No sir. She fell because she is a Malay woman. She met my friend in Belaga. She came to live here because she married an Ukit. She is not used to our customs. She is dying. And she is a woman."

"Jams," said Leon, "if we go to Belaga it will be the ends of our journey. There will be no more petrols. We will not come back."

"Come on," said James, suddenly angry, rabbit-punching the air with his right hand, "I damn well won't stand for it. I will not have the death of this woman on my conscience just to take you on some picnic. It's monstrous. I won't have it."

"You have broken your promise," said the Ukit, disgusted, getting to his feet, turning up the volume on the cassette player and joining the dance with his back to us.

Our hostess emerged from her shadowy corner by the window frame. She slipped down beside James and put her hand on his knee.

"I hear you, tuan," she said. "You kind man. I watch you. Now I make you many rices. My husband, he leave me. He go away downriver. Please, tuan, you give me money for Three Legs? I have headache, always, all the time."

"We have pills for that," I said, about to fetch the vitamin bag.

She held her brow with her free hand.

"No, not white man medicine," she said, "Not orang puteh pills. Three Legs."

James gave her five dollars and she disappeared into the kitchen.

There then came, from beneath us, a loud, insistent banging on the stilts of the hut. The floor we sat on shook with the impacts.

"Jesus," said James, half-joking, "this is when they kill us."

The young Ukit shouted to each other and began to dance with exaggerated vigour. A party of middle-aged men in loincloths, superbly tattooed, nodded a staccato farewell to us and swung themselves out of the window. The banging increased in tempo and each blow became more violent.

"What is it?" said James. "For Chirst's sake—what is it?"

"It's very bads," hissed Leon, tense, his eyes wide, not knowing what to do, glancing first at the window and then at the door, "is trouble."

"Take no notice, sir," said our guide, "it is only the old men. They are ignorant and, actually, they do not like our disco. They want to sleep. But tonight we dance."

"Then turn the bloody thing off," said James, bounding up with explosive and surprising speed towards the cassette recorder. He knocked it over and scrabbled at all its buttons. The tape ejected on to the floor. The music stopped. The banging ceased.

"Please sir, you stay here. I will tell the old men how to behave," said our guide, leaving the room and descending the pole. Everyone else, except the group of young Ukit and one ancient hunter, left smartly by the window, gripping the roof with their bare feet, scuttling along a ledge to the left and disappearing into the night.

From below, there came the sound of raised voices, shouts, the noise of a scuffle, a thump against the stilts; and then all was silent.

Our guide returned, his face dark, his chest and back covered in deep red-brown patches, his eyes full of tears. He spoke fast in Ukit. He was shivering with shock or rage or both. His friends restrained him, the boys holding his arms, hard, and the girls placing their hands on his back and shoulders. The little group stood there, motionless, huddled together under the light of the lamp, and our guide began to be calmed, to breathe regularly.

"They punched me," he said. "They would not listen. Believe me sir, if I had had my spear with me, it would have been different. For once in my life I would like to commit a dark deed. I would like to see the blood spurt from their livers."

"Don't worry," I said, "this happens all the time in Oxford. The dons always beat up the students when a disco goes on after midnight."

"Redmond," said James, "don't make silly jokes. Calm down. Okay?"

Realising, suddenly, that this would be our first and last evening amongst the least-studied of all the jungle nomads I fetched Smythies and Lord Medway's *Mammals of Borneo* from my Bergen. I opened Smythies and laid it on the floor. The healing group broke up and came and sat round us in a circle.

"Do you know all these birds?" I said.

Our battered guide flicked through the pages.

"No sir, actually we young men do not. But this old man here" (he gestured towards the ancient hunter, who was sitting peacefully by himself against the wall with several bottles of Guinness at his side) "he will know them, every one. He is old now. He is stupid. But, in his youth, with the blowpipe, he was the greatest of the Ukit. It is said amongst us, sir, that he ran so fast he could catch the birds in their flight."

Our guide beckoned and the old man shuffled over and sat in front of us. His ears were pierced, and he was tattooed across the shoulders with a series of stars and roundels. James poured a double scotch in a mess-tin and set the offering at his right foot; I pushed Smythies over to his left. He shook his head at the plate of the Bald-headed woodshrike, but then his face crinkled, slowly, into a leathery smile. He turned the pages with bemused delight, mumbling to himself in his own language the names of all the birds of his wandering youth.

Much excited, I opened the *Mammals of Borneo* at Medway's

photograph of the wallowing Borneo rhinoceros, and placed it beside Smythies. The old man stiffened. His thumb came down on the page with a crack. He turned to our guide, his face alert, his thin muscles bunched, and he talked with a wild intensity.

"He wishes to tell you, sir," said our guide, "that when he was young, when he was a man just like us, by the mountain known as Tiban, he killed eight of these with his own best spear." Our search had ended.

• SELECT BIBLIOGRAPHY •

Baring-Gould, S., and C. A. Bampfylde, *A History of Sarawak under its Two White Rajahs 1839–1908*, London, 1909.

Beccari, Odoardo, *Wanderings in the Great Forests of Borneo, Travels and Researches of a Naturalist in Sarawak*, trans Enrico H. Giglioli, ed F. H. H. Guillemard, London, 1904.

Brooke, Charles A. J., *Ten Years in Sarawak*, 2 vols, London, 1866.

Brothwell, D. R., "Upper Pleistocene Human Skull from Niah Caves", *The Sarawak Museum Journal*, vol IX, July–December 1960, pps 323–49.

Burgess, P. F., "Breeding of the White-bellied Swiflet (*Collocalia esculenta*)", *The Sarawak Museum Journal*, vol X, July–December 1961, pps 264–9.

Childe, V. Gordon, "'Long Houses' of Prehistoric Europe", *The Sarawak Museum Journal*, vol VII, December 1956, pps 259–62.

Chin, Lucas, *Cultural Heritage of Sarawak*, Kuching, 1980.

Conrad, J., "Heart of Darkness", *Blackwood's Magazine*, Feb–April, 1899. *Youth, a Narrative; and Two Other Stories*, Edinburgh and London, 1902.
"Lord Jim; a Tale", *Blackwood's Magazine*, Oct 1899–Nov 1900; *Lord Jim; a Tale*, Edinburgh, London, New York and Toronto, 1900.

Crisswell, Colin N., *Rajah Charles Brooke, Monarch of all he Surveyed*, Kuala Lumpur, 1978.

Darlington, C. D., *The Evolution of Man and Society*, London, 1969.

Darwin, C., *On the Origin of Species by Means of Natural Selection, or the Preservation of Favoured Races in the Struggle for Life*, London, 1859.
The Descent of Man and Selection in Relation to Sex, London, 2 vols, 1871.

Dickens, Peter, *SAS, the Jungle Frontier, 22 Special Air Service Regiment in the Borneo Campaign, 1963–1966*, London, 1983.

Fraser, J. G., *The Golden Bough: a Study in Comparative Religion*, 2 vols, London 1890.

Freeman, J. D., *Iban Agriculture, a Report on the Shifting Cultivation of Hill Rice by the Iban of Sarawak*, London, 1955.
"Iban Augury", in Bertram E. Smythies, *The Birds of Borneo*, Edinburgh, 1960, pps 73–98.
"A Note on the Gawai Kenyalang, or Hornbill Ritual of the Iban of Sarawak", in Bertram E. Smythies, *The Birds of Borneo*, Edinburgh, 1960, pps 99–102.

Galton, Francis, *The Art of Travel; or, Shifts and Contrivances Available in Wild Countries*, London, 1855.

Geddes, W. R., *Nine Dayak Nights*, Melbourne, 1957.

George, Wilma, *Biologist Philosopher, a Study of the Life and Writings of Alfred Russel Wallace*, London, 1964.

Geraghty, Tony, *Who Dares Wins, the Story of the Special Air Service 1950–1980*, London, 1980.

Gimlette, John D., *Malay Poisons and Charm Cures*, Kuala Lumpur, 1915.

Glenister, A. G., *The Birds of the Malay Peninsula, Singapore and Penang, an Account of all the Malayan Species, with a Note of their Occurrence in SUMATRA, BORNEO, and JAVA and a List of the Birds of those Islands*, Kuala Lumpur, 1951.

Haddon, Alfred C., and Laura Start, *Iban or Sea Dayak Fabrics and their Patterns, a Descriptive Catalogue of the Iban Fabrics in the Museum of Archaeology and Ethnology Cambridge*, Cambridge, 1936.

Hanbury-Tenison, Robin, *Mulu, the Rain Forest*, London, 1980.

Harrison, John, *An Introduction to Mammals of Singapore and Malaya*, Singapore, 1974.

Harrisson, Barbara, "Orang-utan: what chances of Survival?", *The Sarawak Museum Journal*, vol X, July–December 1961, pps 238–61.

"A Classification of Stone Age Burials from Niah Great Cave, Sarawak", *The Sarawak Museum Journal*, vol XV, July–December 1967, pps 126–200.

Harrisson, Tom, "Rhinoceros in Borneo: and Traded to China", *The Sarawak Museum Journal*, vol VII, December 1956, pps 263–74.

"The caves of Niah: a History of Prehistory", *The Sarawak Museum Journal*, vol VIII, December 1958, pps 549–95.

World Within, a Borneo Story, London, 1959.

"Birds and Men in Borneo", in Bertram E. Smythies, *The Birds of Borneo*, Edinburgh, 1960, pps 20–62.

"Borneo Bird Notes, 1966–7 from Various Hands", compiled by Tom Harrisson, *The Sarawak Museum Journal*, vol XV, July–December 1967, pps 414–23.

Harrisson, Tom and Stephen Wan Ullok, "A Sarawak Kenyah Journey through Death", *The Sarawak Museum Journal*, vol X, July–December 1961, pps 191–213.

Hatt, John, *The Tropical Traveller*, London, 1982.

Hose, Charles, *The Field-book of a Jungle-Wallah, Being a Description of Shore, River and Forest Life in Sarawak*, London, 1929.

Hose, Charles, and William McDougall, *The Pagan Tribes of Borneo, a Description of their Physical, Moral and Intellectual Condition with some Discussion of their Ethnic Relations, with an Appendix on the Physical Characters of the Races of Borneo by A. C. Haddon*, 2 vols, London, 1912.

Keppel, Henry, *The Expedition to Borneo of HMS Dido for the Suppression of Piracy, with Extracts from the Journal of James Brooke Esq*, 2 vols, London, 1846.

King, Ben F., and Edward C. Dickinson, *A Field Guide to the Birds of South-East Asia, Covering Burma, Malaya, Thailand, Cambodia, Vietnam, Laos and Hong Kong*, London, 1975.

King, Victor T., *Essays on Borneo Societies*, Oxford, 1978.

Law, C. P., "Chinese Temples in Kuching—II", *The Sarawak Museum Journal*, vol IX, July–December 1959, pps 47–8.

186

Levien, Michael, *The Cree Journals, the Voyages of Edward H. Cree, Surgeon RN, as Related in His Private Journals, 1837–1856*, Exeter, 1981.

Lubbock, Sir John, *Pre-Historic Times, as Illustrated by Ancient Remains in the Manners and Customs of Modern Savages*, London, 1865.

The Origin of Civilisation and the Primitive Condition of Man, Mental and Social Condition of Savages, London, 1870.

Luping, Datin Margaret, and Chin Wen and E. Richard Dingley, eds, *Kinabalu, Summit of Borneo*, Kota Kinabalu, 1978.

Macdonald, David, *Expedition to Borneo, the Search for Proboscis Monkeys and other creatures*, London, 1982.

Macdonald, Malcolm, *Borneo People*, London, 1956.

Marchant, James, ed, Alfred Russel Wallace, *Letters and Reminiscences*, 2 vols, London, 1916.

Maxwell, Sir George, *In Malay Forests*, London, 1908.

Mayr, Ernst, *Birds of the Southwest Pacific, a Field Guide to the Birds of the Area between Samoa, New Caledonia, and Micronesia*, New York, 1945.

Lord Medway, *Mammals of Borneo, Field Keys and an annotated Checklist*, Kuala Lumpur, 1965.

Metcalf, Peter, *A Borneo Journey into Death, Berawan Eschatology from its Rituals*, Philadelphia, 1982.

Payne, Robert, *The White Rajahs of Sarawak*, London, 1960.

Pringle, Robert, *Rajahs and Rebels, the Ibans of Sarawak under Brooke Rule, 1841–1941*, London, 1970.

Roth, Henry Ling, *The Natives of Sarawak and British North Borneo*, 2 vols, London, 1896.

Rubenstein, Carol, "Poems of Indigenous Peoples of Sarawak: Some of the songs and chants", *The Sarawak Museum Journal, Special Monograph No 2*, vol XXI, parts I and II, July 1973.

Runciman, Steven, *The White Rajahs, a History of Sarawak from 1841 to 1946*, Cambridge, 1960.

St John, Spenser, *Life in the Forests of the Far East; or Travels in Northern Borneo*, 2 vols, London, 1862.

The Life of Sir James Brooke, Rajah of Sarawak, London, 1879.

Sandin, Benedict, "Cock-Fighting: the Dayak National Game", *The Sarawak Museum Journal*, vol IX, July–December 1959, pps 25–32.

Shelford, Robert W. C., *A Naturalist in Borneo*, ed by Edward B. Poulton, London, 1916.

Smythies, Bertram E., *The Birds of Borneo*, Edinburgh, 1960; third edition, Kuala Lumpur, 1981.

"An Annotated Checklist of the Birds of Borneo", *The Sarawak Museum Journal*, vol VII, June 1957, pps i–818.

Templer, John C. (ed.), *The Private Letters of Sir James Brooke, KCB, Rajah of Sarawak, Narrating the Events of his Life, from 1863 to the Present Time*, 3 vols, London, 1853.

Tweedie, M. W. F., *Common Birds of the Malay Peninsula*, Kuala Lumpur, 1970.

Tweedie, M. W. F., and J. L. Harrison, *Malayan Animal Life*, Kuala Lumpur, 1954.

Tylor, Edward B., *Researches into the Early History of Mankind and the Development of Civilisation*, London, 1865.

Primitive Culture: Researches into the Development of Mythology, Philosophy, Religion, Art and Custom, 2 vols, London, 1871.

Wallace, Alfred Russel, *The Malay Archipelago: the Land of the Orang-Utan and the Bird of Paradise. A Narrative of Travel, with Studies of man and nature*, 2 vols, London, 1869.

Island Life: or, the Phenomena and Causes of Insular Faunas and Floras; Including a Revision and Attempted Solution of the Problem of Geological Climates, London, 1880.

Natural Selection and Tropical Nature, essays on Descriptive and Theoretical Biology, London, 1891 (*Natural Selection*, first ed, London 1870; *Tropical Nature*, first ed, London, 1878).

Warner, Philip, *The SAS*, London, 1971.

· INDEX ·

Compiled by Douglas Matthews

In addition to *No Mercy* and *In Trouble Again*,
Redmond O'Hanlon has published scholarly works
on nineteenth-century science and literature. For
many years the natural history editor of the *Times
Literary Supplement,* he lives outside Oxford with
his wife and two children.